Design for Gardens

Design for Gardens

Joseph Hudak

TIMBER PRESS
Portland, Oregon

Published in 2000 by
Timber Press, Inc.
The Haseltine Building
133 S.W. Second Avenue, Suite 450
Portland, Oregon 97204, U.S.A.

Printed in Hong Kong

Designed by Susan Applegate

Library of Congress Cataloging-in-Publication Data

Hudak, Joseph.
Design for gardens/Joseph Hudak
     p.   cm.
ISBN 0-88192-441-5
1. Gardens—Design. 2. Plants, Ornamental. I. Title.
SB473.H83 2000
712'.6–dc21   99-39196
                                                    CIP

To all who delight in the design of gardens
from the past, for the present, and into the future

Contents

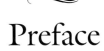

Preface

All my previous hardcover books focused on major plant categories for themselves. First came *Gardening with Perennials Month by Month* followed by *Trees for Every Purpose* and then *Shrubs in the Landscape*. I recently updated and expanded the perennials book for its second edition with Timber Press, and my improved version of the shrub book is also due in the near future.

The present book is far different in scope since it explores the compositional uses of plants in garden designs along with the interaction of outdoor spaces and construction elements used by homeowners. It is fully intended for an international audience because the principles of garden design are not bound by any specific geographic locales. We all are somewhat limited, however, by climate, soil type, and plant hardiness in achieving our personal expressions for any garden layout, and so we obviously need to analyze and reanalyze our situation from time to time. Every gardener inevitably "borrows" some appealing ideas from a number of existing projects with amazing ease and zest, which makes the many garden developments by homeowners truly remarkable exercises of versatility and adaptability.

As a landscape architect with more than forty-five years of professional practice stretching from Maine to Florida, to parts of the Midwest and even southeastern Canada, I have consistently applied the objectives of garden design presented in this book to assist thousands of clients improve their home grounds. As a lifelong working gardener I have also experienced firsthand the great joys and awful dismays of a wealth of plants grown for my own pleasure as well as for that of my clients. Practical, hands-on involvement is a great teacher but a hard taskmaster.

In this book I explain the essential design guidelines in substantial but user-friendly ways, so the data contribute many practical aspects as well. My hope is that such shared information will prove valuable not only for those currently involved with remodeling or creating gardens but also for those who just enjoy admiring them for their artistic merits.

To provide additional guidance beyond the text, I have selected photos from my personal collection illustrating actual landscape situations. Line drawings are not included because to me color photos provide a far more useful expression of detail, spatial depth, and garden meaning. Planting plans are also omitted since they are truly functional only when designed for specific sites and particular growing conditions. In a book with this broad scope, no special planting arrangement could possibly be of use for every reader.

The final chapter presents a step-by-step history of a personal five-year garden design project at my second Massachusetts home involving the rear portion of a one-third-acre lot in suburbia. The finished result earned an eight-page photo essay in a national magazine. May this effort provide encouragement to other do-it-yourselfers.

I trust the information and format of the book will supply enough motivation and direction for you to interpret your own garden design ideas with greater assurance and satisfaction. You take up a fascinating challenge when making a garden of any size, and you should not only draw on your own intelligence and experience but on that of others as well, since gardens are pleasure grounds without boundaries for ideas.

Introduction

When you commit to creating a garden your main goal should be to produce a coordinated, comfortable, and convenient outdoor series of spaces for your personal use and enjoyment. Garden-makers around the world have supported this same sense of clear purpose for centuries, and today's enthusiasts are just as determined to achieve such results. Having a well-structured program in place before you begin will be a great aid.

The principal element of garden design is, of course, the plant material, with its unique ability as a living entity to expand annually and to please us with a myriad of useful and attractive values throughout the seasons. Except for the effects of weathering, garden structures such as walls, fences, terraces, decks, or walkways remain basically the same size and color over time. This means that two importantly different systems are at work in most garden design exercises: the living and the inert. Blending them successfully in true harmony takes skill and persistence.

Although the styles of our gardens are continually altered to reflect the revised wants and needs of each era, the practical purposes of planting do not vary much. Today we install all types of plant material to provide essential shade, privacy screening, erosion and dust control, sound baffling, and wind protection, just as every generation before us has done—and as others will surely do in the future.

Unchanged, too, are the sensory and ornamental functions of garden planting, with the welcome contributions of color, fragrance, texture, form, and movement. Combining the practical aspects with these aesthetic features into an attractive picture is what successful residential garden design is all about. Its aim, then, is to blend all kinds of history, horticulture, and home styles into a welcoming arrangement with enduring appeal. When well done it can only grow in visual value.

As our social attitudes fluctuate over a lifetime, our focus in garden interpretations will also follow suit. Just as architectural modes vary beguilingly from one historic period to another, so too our remodeling of garden spaces accompanies these trends into new areas of expression. Add to this reorganization the zeal of plant hybridizers seeking to keep the public constantly dazzled with improved plant choices, and we discover that some new and stimulating way of assembling plant types is on the horizon of every garden designer, whether professional or amateur.

The land surrounding a private residence is normally organized to enhance one family's needs, and this personal emphasis provides a wealth of garden design opportunities not only for a definitive point of view but for special refinement in all the details. A homeowner's treatment of the grounds, then, is frequently interpreted as a public display of his or her own lifestyle. That can be quite a responsibility.

Successful gardens, however, are not just made by physical actions but are fully imagined well before the first shovel of earth is turned. Any enduring design results from much concentrated thinking beforehand toward resolving site problems intelligently while also creating personal and meaningful benefits. Sorry to say, I can offer no magic formula here that will outperform your thinking ahead. Without a well-conceived plan of achievable goals from the start, you might end up wandering inconclusively—and probably expensively—with your time, effort, and money. If you do not intend to proceed that way, then you have to plan a rewarding program first.

Whether you garden in the city, suburbs, seashore, or mountaintop, set aside enough time to prepare a comprehensive general outline for the development of your entire site. You will soon like—or even dislike—the many parts more fully when you bring together your separate ideas for each area into a single outline. Such simple organization of your ideas is far superior, and cheaper, than physically rearranging your grounds on a whim.

All of us can benefit from focused, time-tested recommendations based on personal experience—our own as well as from others we admire—and my aim in this book is to provide long-established principles of garden design that have guided my own approaches for design solutions. Some of these guidelines are conspicuously simple and others are more complex, yet all are valuable in some degree for achieving true garden harmony. Always keep in mind that the art of garden making rests as much on your good use of intelligent ideas as on your critical evaluation of the combinations you arrange.

Granted, your local climate, soil type, range of plant hardiness, and available time for needed maintenance will always play vital roles in your final design resolution. Yet whether you are an avid do-it-yourselfer or a whiz at coaxing a local contractor to fulfill your wishes to perfection, the creation of a rewarding garden setting will develop more satisfactorily when you understand and apply the information offered here. These design recommendations can truly expand your garden pleasures.

Although this book is mainly a garden primer for planting design, other important site adjustments will surely be needed at some point as well. If you value the proposed planting layout as the icing on the cake, be certain that the cake (or site) is well organized beforehand. For example, contour grading to establish level areas for play or display, clearing of nonessential plants or rock formations, and modifying unsatisfactory surface-water drainage, along with building construction essentials such as a retaining wall, a paved terrace, a screen fence, or a swimming pool, are all conspicuous features of site renovations, too. These non-planting aspects are addressed throughout the book as substantially useful elements for harmonizing the entire garden picture.

Keep in mind that time is an intrinsic part of all garden planting efforts. Your permanent woody material will enlarge and definitely modify the original design concept over the years. It is always worthwhile to learn beforehand the expected mature size and annual growth rate of your selections. Simply put: "know it before you grow it." This valuable knowledge will allow you to avoid the burden of surprisingly rapid overgrowth, eventual crowding, and the costly effort for removals and replanting with more suitable choices. When you begin well, you will end well. I trust this book will prove a faithful, practical, and useful guide for your fascinating journey.

Chapter 1

Gardening Innovations Through the Centuries

Learning when and where enduring garden ideas first came into play has consistently been revealing and certainly intriguing. Explore with me, then, the history of some time-honored innovations. While there may seem to be little really new under the sun nowadays, it can still be surprising to discover the origins of gardening practices and design ideas we simply take for granted. If there is a specific horticultural benefit that you wish to achieve in your garden, you will probably find hints or solutions from nearly any century or culture. An ancient practice, reinterpreted for today's use, might well become an original enterprise.

Gardens have been associated with human development since the beginning of our earthly existence, and we still pursue two long-lasting values from our outdoor environment: usefulness and beauty. The desire to be surrounded by plants is instinctive in humans, whether the plants are presented as Nature intended or as we believe they should be set out in particular designs. In Western culture, the first garden is described in the Bible as Eden, where everything was in perfect harmony and plants blossomed and fruited continuously without handicaps. This paradise did not endure long, unfortunately, and humanity continues to struggle daily against myriad obstacles in an effort to tame the natural wilderness for personal use and satisfaction.

No gardens of our earliest history survive today, of course, but we can gain some inkling about their value and expression from fragmented descriptions in hieroglyphics, writings, tapestries, and unearthed ruins. These ancient sources reflect the cultures of long-vanished civilizations and attest to the importance of garden making throughout time. It certainly is valid and profitable for us to learn where humans have been before we go forward with any assurance that we can improve on the past. What follows are some highlights of previous garden creativity, and these concepts of the distant past are still enjoyed in some modified form today. Any good idea has amazing persistence.

Ancient civilizations quickly established that not only did an earthly paradise require plants that reliably nourish the body but also that other plants have merit for their shade, as wind barriers for crops and livestock, and as construction timber. Naturally, a generous and continual source of pure drinking water, channeled further for irrigation and cooling, was also a high priority for locating any dwelling and its garden. In every long-gone society, garden spaces were ornamented in an individualistic fashion—just as we all do today. Since our attitudes and needs constantly change, our garden developments naturally follow suit.

Thousands of years ago the Egyptians built stout walls of mud, brick, and, later, stone around their symmetrical, utilitarian food plots and adjacent homes as protection against the incessant drying winds howling from the featureless desert. These barriers also served well to protect the inhabitants and their crops from packs of wild, foraging animals and human enemies. Eventually these simple outposts grew into generous settlements, and in these secure and permanent communities people began constructing interior, palm-shaded courtyards for leisure and social entertaining to escape the oppressive heat and dust. These garden surroundings often contained fragrant vines, tightly pruned shrubs, and colorful, tubbed flowers near a long, rectangular, and decorative pool of still water. Gardening as an art form now had its cohesive beginning.

Ancient Greeks defined a garden as *hortus,* meaning "enclosure," from which the term *horticulture,* the practice of garden tending, can easily be traced. They also established the first roof gardens with sizable clay pots and wood tubs once the open, tillable land of the city became scarce in the midst of a local geography known for its many rugged, almost treeless mountains and skimpy soil cover. Later generations of early Greeks are credited with developing intelligent city planning by their practice of installing large quantities of shade trees throughout various urban spaces for improved human comfort and civic beauty. This occurred a thousand years before any other nearby civilization gave this idea any merit. Yet another point of civic concern stressed by these ancient Greeks was placing important buildings on high, dominating sites that possessed the most suitable prospects for anticipated expansion later. Recognizing the natural distinction of a site for special development is still a valid landscape focus even today.

The later empire-building Romans—never averse to absorbing and enhancing any attractive idea from the diverse cultures they came to control—celebrated their own pleasantly mild, but dry, Mediterranean climate with spacious outdoor terraces, interior courtyards open to the sky, generous passageways festooned with scented vines, and extensive water features. The Romans greatly valued their skill at water engineering and used it importantly by constructing water-supply aqueducts, public baths, and civic fountains wherever they expanded their territories. Some of these aqueducts still function today.

Ancient hilltop ruins in Athens, Greece.

Within their homes the Romans visually enlarged the interior spaces by incorporating either large wall mosaics or paintings of idealized landscape scenes. Their main outdoor garden plants were selected to be both evergreen and highly aromatic, and this normally included extensive use of orange and bay trees—with some espaliered flat against walls—along with myrtle, thyme, and rosemary as fillers on the ground or in pots.

Ornamental horticulture thrived and expanded for generations in the durable Roman Empire and soon included hothouses called *specularia* for growing exotic melons and rare flowers out of season. Because glass could not be manufactured in large sheets at that time, the roofs of these *specularia* were composed of wafer-thin sections of talc, which is reasonably transparent when sliced.

The shearing of garden plants into architectural forms became such an art with the Romans that the higher grade of slave who tended these special plants

A replica of an early Roman interior garden, Pompeii, Italy.

An ancient Roman interior wall mosaic of landscape scenes, Herculaneum, Italy.

was called a *topiarius,* from which the contemporary *topiary* has its origins. Pliny, in his writings about Roman life several thousand years ago, included descriptions of sizable window boxes planted in a variety of compelling ways at many homes and public buildings.

In 476 A.D. the widespread Roman civilization collapsed to marauding Goths from northern Europe, and this defeat lead to a slow but consistent disintegration of known governmental order as well as of maintenance for paved roads, aqueducts, and life-sustaining farms that had unified the Empire across most of Europe and the British Isles. This was the grim start to nearly five centuries of social and political insecurity known as the Dark Ages.

Unfortunately for the progress of humanity, this period of decay and withdrawal forced the isolation of horticulture and gardening ideas as well. The precious knowledge about plant life went into seclusion behind the fortified monastery walls of Christian religious organizations, which became major forces in agriculture as well as the main guardians of salvaged past knowledge in many fields of learning in the West. Within these monastery walls a pressing

An elaborate hemlock topiary screen in Maryland.

need for self-sufficiency led to a practical focus on medicinal herb and vegetable gardening, effectively managed either by constricted, in-ground plots or in low, raised troughs made of stone or wood often set right on the upper level, flat flooring of the building itself. Eventually, plants grown for the flowers used in chapel decorations—a practice some lay members of the community thought far too heathenish to endorse—also appeared within the vegetable patches. When there was sufficient root room, small-sized fruit trees for making preserves were added to the plant collection. When gardening space was constricted, however, these productive trees were carefully trained as espaliers to grow flat against sunny wall exposures. Every age has its practical wizards.

In these garden spaces a generous source of water was always conveniently close at hand. It might be a large, open tub with live fish made available for the meatless Friday meals. Another would be a central, bubbling fountain providing the main water source for drinking, bathing, and plant watering with buck-

A medieval-style in-ground herb garden, England.

ets. Eventually this well water was diverted into complex runs for more efficient irrigation of the expanding food crops. Yet even though this well-managed system proved its worth, it remained isolated from the rest of humanity until at least 1000 A.D. Life outside monastery walls until then was highly unpredictable.

By the eleventh century the European age of chivalry, or the medieval era, had emerged, and private fortified castle grounds offered outdoor scenes for courtly promenading, for games and dancing, for reading and sewing, or for wooing, all out of view behind massive stone walls. Large ornamental fountains, decorative arbors hung with scented vines, and awninged pavilions brightened the interior surroundings, while fragrant-blooming trees, caged song birds, and turf-topped, brick benches covered attractively with delicate wildflowers and small bulbs poking through the grass were commonplace. The addition of fresh garden odors—at least in the growing season—helped to counterbalance the smelly and damp confines of these stone citadels, which housed a large number of both noisy humans and various livestock in extremely close proximity. While this living arrangement may seem romantic to some today, it was nearly chaotic to the inhabitants a millennium ago. Everyone benefits with separate spaces for business and pleasure.

During medieval times the cloister garden of covered passageways with colonnaded openings toward a trickling central fountain was modified to feature, instead, a parterre or geometric, flattened outline of interconnected, squared or curved sections neatly bordered with low, clipped hedges. These framed a decorative interior space covered with a carpet of either colored pebbles, broken brick, or sand. More elaborate designs often reproduced the owner's coat of arms and were best viewed, of course, from an upper castle window to capture all the detailing. This noticeable garden display contributed year-long appeal and was especially rewarding for those rising up in the chain of command.

The labyrinth was another popular garden novelty in the late Middle Ages. This planting device dates back to the Cretan civilization of 2000 B.C. and the mythological adventures of Ariadne, who used a spindle of twine to lead her lover, Theseus, out of the confusion of the labyrinth. Whether square, round, or rectangular in outline, a labyrinth provides perplexing fun for uninitiated participants by its intentionally baffling interior pattern of tall, screening, clipped hedges between gravel paths that frequently lead pointedly to a dead

A twelfth-century moated castle at Bodiam, England.

An eighteenth-century Spanish cloister garden in Santa Barbara, California.

end. Intended as a puzzle with many possible routes to intensify the disorientation and playfulness of the scheme, labyrinths have been employed in gardens up through the present day.

For similar if lower-keyed game playing, a maze of paths was laid out in a more easily comprehended, often circular design, with one route leading to the center and back out again—but not directly. There were still dead ends but far fewer choices to bother anyone, especially since the design was made of low hedge borders that enclosed either narrow flower beds or colored stones and could be skipped over readily to shorten the solution. A maze offered more contemplative, social strolling as well as a large and neatly framed garden ornament. In later times it evolved into a complex patterning of just interwoven evergreen hedges of strictly visual interest. Such a show is more an architectural layout and display of pruning skill than a presentation of plants for their own sakes. The upkeep, of course, is extravagantly costly and time-consuming.

A nineteenth-century formal maze, Portugal.

In the fourteenth century the adventuresome Marco Polo of Venice wrote of his many lengthy journeys to remote China. He revealed how the highly conservative leaders of this unique civilization had for thousands of years maintained a far simpler approach to garden design than had been imagined by Europeans. Polo described in detail the Chinese technique of constructing rectangular walled spaces adjacent to their homes and temples, creating many rabbit-warren-size areas of personalized interest. Here they emphasized the symbolic importance of unusual rocks, water islands, and just a few intriguingly shaped trees or shrubs set, perhaps, in beds of moss. The Chinese considered such basic, natural elements to be the only essential ingredients for successful and mind-stimulating gardening. To them garden artistry was valued as a logical branch of landscape painting, only expressed in three dimensions.

Frequently such Chinese gardens feature a viewing pavilion in a large enclosure, and instead of fixed benches they offer portable, lightweight seating of

An Oriental-style viewing pavilion and garden, San Marino, California.

Chinese movable glazed-pottery seating.

A Japanese-style sand garden in San Marino, California.

glazed pottery in several locations about the setting. This movability allows for individual resting spots throughout the garden for quietly observing special moments of the changing seasons. Private contemplation for the Chinese held great meaning hundreds of years ago, as it still does today.

In later decades these early Chinese garden interpretations crossed over to Japan, but there the basic garden principles of mood creation were expanded to encompass the deliberate use of distinct opposites or sharp contrasts balanced with each other. In Japanese garden layouts, smooth objects played against gnarled ones, straight lines opposed curved shapes, and dappled light contrasted with nearby brightness. Subtle meanings from the landscape were soon the established norm for gardens.

The Japanese also formulated the unique raked-sand garden design, which imitated the many beguiling aspects of water movement. Integrated as a background in some of these sand spaces were a few intricately shaped rocks, often with see-through openings, cut-stone lanterns, a dipping bowl of water for refreshment, and only a selected few specimen plants. It all was intended to form a miniature version of a larger natural scene that the particular designer cherished and wished to repeat for remembered personal pleasure. Such subtleness was then—and often is today—almost incomprehensible to Western thinking, and a greater knowledge of these venerable Asian garden styles did not foster much European interest until well into the eighteenth century, when chinoiserie became a widespread interior-design and garden fad. Various elements of both Chinese and Japanese design concepts were appropriated, but highly modified, to European tastes (and they traveled to the American colonies as well) as desirable novelties without the Oriental philosophies that created them. East does not always meet West successfully.

By 1400 the Italian Renaissance began blossoming throughout all the arts in Florence. A primary pursuit of this humanistic movement was the rediscovery of the natural world and the logical place for humans within it. Fortunately at this point of history some reliable semblance of civic order produced peaceful cooperation in most of Europe, and the new cultural search spurred by the Renaissance was enthusiastically directed outward for generations in a world now actively demanding greater order, reason, and enrichment in all areas of life.

This movement was based on rekindled admiration for ancient Greece, and from that older period the Italian leaders of the sixteenth century resurrected the premise of city planning which held that prominent buildings should be provided with only the most attractive and spacious surroundings. For the first time since the era of the early Caesars, estate builders fully coordinated their palatial hilltop villas with extensive and elaborate walled gardens of mostly geometric designs that flowed magnificently down the surrounding hillsides.

Because of the steep terrain surrounding these palatial residences, broad stone staircases with ornamental balustrades heavily decorated with various statuary became an important design development, leading visitors to wide landings overlooking panoramic views. Lawns and flower beds were largely omitted due to their constant high-watering needs in this dry atmosphere, and the terraces were set, instead, with intricate floor designs of geometrically cut stone or embedded pebbles. Once scorned as too common for garden use, the native plants readily tolerant of parched, hot summers were collected generously and exhibited as functional and artistic background screens. Topiary plants were also promoted and extensively displayed. In grand gestures that only the very powerful and wealthy can create and support even today, natural water runs were diverted and skillfully engineered to produce spectacular and awe-inspiring fountain and waterfall displays.

Now began a lengthy period of dazzling, yet orderly, extravagance in Italian architecture and garden making that was greatly admired by princely visitors and local businesspeople alike, who sought to duplicate these ideas in the expansion of their own grounds. But word of these showplaces traveled widely, and the prominence of these Italian creations was soon completely overshadowed in shear size and elaborateness by those of the grandiose kings of neighboring France. Europe was about to see munificence beyond anyone's imagining.

With much flatter acreage and far larger estate holdings, the French royalty of the seventeenth century expressed its garden embellishments with creativity on a truly spectacular scale. Disregarding cost and the years of intense labor necessary for completion, the nobles leveled forests to form broad, mile-long, axial vistas that carried the eye to the distant horizon from the gigantic palace windows. Adjacent terraces spread out over an acre or more to accommodate hundreds of promenading guests. Dense borders of closely pruned trees acted as sylvan backdrops for sumptuous waterworks or theatrical productions. Enormous lagoons dotted the grounds, with full-sized ships lazily sailing in formation alongside the strolling courtiers. Color and heady fragrance came from extensive parterre layouts of summertime flowers, the particular arrangement of which was often changed overnight at the command of the king. And acres of hand-trimmed lawn completed an exhibition of royal exuberance for breathtaking grounds.

The awesome construction works and fantastic planting displays of Louis XIV at Versailles instilled envy in every other European monarch, inspiring a frenzy of garden-making superlatives never again accomplished on this scale by so many royal houses. Fortunately a large number of these palatial settings are in remarkably restored condition for your inspection today, and they remain highly memorable, if foot-wearying, panoramas of extraordinary garden dom-

The sixteenth-century Neptune fountain at Villa d'Este, Italy.

inance that fully banished naturalism for generations. Artificiality reigned supreme.

In the Great Britain of Henry VIII and his immediate successors, however, there was much less interest in imitating such expensive and pompous garden layouts so avidly pursued on the Continent. Instead, British nobility embraced the simpler horticultural ideas of their valuable trading partner, Holland. British gardens of the time copied the more humanistic Dutch, with gardens crisply enclosed by tall, brick walls or sizable clipped hedges, sporting within them box-bordered flower beds, herbal knot gardens, and sundials or armillaries instead of central fountains, along with myriad bowling greens and mazes. The British prided themselves in continual and personal involvement with their pleasure grounds by regularly walking or riding through their properties rather than just admiring them only as showcases viewed from a fixed point. That tradition continues today.

A replica of a sixteenth-century knot garden in England.

By the eighteenth century, however, the formal garden layouts on British estates were challenged by the pronouncements of two Englishmen who gained the keen attention of landed gentry favoring some new innovations. An orientation toward naturalistic landscapes was vigorously championed first by Lancelot Brown, who became fashionably known as "Capability" for his constant statements in speech and print of the inherent *capabilities* of a site, which would be properly released only if his ideas were followed. He was followed in later decades by a similar proponent of the natural landscape treatment, Humphry Repton. Both men emphatically believed that the finest landscape creation was the one that naturally appeared to have always been there. Each designer found both fond supporters as well as angry critics among the British landowners of the times, but a major renovation of garden design was underway, with important influences still echoing into our own era.

For Brown, any house foundation planting or flower garden was completely dismissed as intrusive to the setting, and he proposed that only mowed lawn should run right up to the building. Carriage drives and walkways now became both contour-hugging and meanderingly serpentine instead of ramrod-straight as before. Sheep, cattle, or deer herds on these massive estates were allowed to graze freely into many of the created vistas, while large water ponds, both naturally existing and man-made, were strongly emphasized as attractive reflecting basins for the sweeps of adjacent scenery.

Brown endorsed a picturesque, but austere, approach to pastoral scenery based on his own personal, emotional responses to Nature. He installed grand sweeps of grass—both mowed, either by herds of sheep or by human-powered scythes, and unmowed, to wave gracefully in the breezes—together with large clumps of newly planted trees (from a surprisingly small list of exclusively native types) in all manufactured views. He resolutely refused, however, to allow even a single flower bed or formal layout to interrupt his creations. Here was the beginning of the naturalistic, parklike estate in a more relaxed association with Nature that soon had widespread appeal with the gentry.

Repton, on the other hand, formulated a bit later the eclectic idea of "the best from anywhere and everywhere" and recommended exotic plant material, combined with suitable local types, in highly conspicuous but practical and tasteful arrangements. To Repton we owe the origin of the term "landscape gardener," a name he selected to show the logical union of the scientific resources of a landscape painter with the abilities of a practical and resourceful gardener. Repton strategically arranged groups of trees throughout his commissioned designs in a freer, more relaxed style to provide horticultural frames for distant, attractive views. He also designed his planting schemes to form entrancing effects of light and shade and new perspectives of the grounds in all seasons.

All these changes in garden-estate design were part of a popular movement called Romanticism, which saw the return of wonder and imaginative sensitivity to all types of artistic expression. It led to the exaltation of the primitive and the recognition of the common man along with a favoring of melancholy in a reaction against the strict forms and rules of the earlier neoclassicism. Tumbled columns and stone building ruins were actually created to aid this mood even if they had no prior relationship to the setting.

With the sudden influx of novel plant material introduced to British gardens from overseas exploration, plus the appearance of greenhouses (originally called "stoves") to care for the more tender ones, Repton graciously "allowed" the return of limited flower borders as well as beds of hardy flowering shrubs in areas

An eighteenth-century English country manor, exhibiting the extensive open views favored by Lancelot Brown.

close to formal outdoor terraces. He also became a master of elaborate trellis design and of enclosed garden spaces for showing off a client's horticultural rarities.

Repton's pastoral landscape theory that "all Nature is a garden" soon became widely accepted on the Continent as well and led to the establishment of public botanic gardens and public parks for all to admire and use for their own garden projects. These displays introduced people of every social level to new approaches toward combining plants, and these influences, of course, attracted similar horticultural interest in the United States by the beginning of the nineteenth century.

Back in seventeenth- and eighteenth-century colonial America, however, the struggle for mere survival kept gardens highly utilitarian and basic, especially in the harsh climate of the early settlements of the northern coastal regions, where gardening space was never given over for display alone. Here the

A replica of a seventeenth-century herb garden at Plimoth Plantation, Massachusetts.

planted areas were tended strictly for food supplies and for medicinal or flavoring herbs and shrubs. Flowers were incidental attractions, and it was not until the middle of the eighteenth century that more decorative uses of plants became widely evident.

During these same times the southern American colonies presented a different landscape picture, where the more genteel social atmosphere, generous land holdings of richly productive soil, and a milder climate allowed for grander garden improvements far earlier. Managed by large numbers of African slaves or indentured servants from Europe, the plantation estates of Virginia and those farther south along the eastern seaboard were located close to major rivers for easier commercial or social travels, since interconnecting roads were few and far between. Such land holdings often displayed largely open lawns dotted only with occasional specimen trees directing the eye prominently to the important waterfront landing dock.

A formal garden based on eighteenth-century Dutch designs, Williamsburg, Virginia.

Garden spaces near the mansions often were reproductions based on the British heritage of the original settlers and often featured geometric patterns of boxwood hedges. Walls of locally formed brick or wood fencing with fanciful designs usually screened or divided parts of these outdoor social or utilitarian areas. In colonial Williamsburg, for example, every house plot was required by law to be fully bordered by either fencing or high walls, mainly to restrict wandering livestock from intruding into a neighbor's land.

Following the Revolutionary War a general mood for living well brought a bonanza of new construction with more elaborate homes and their inevitable formal gardens. The styles of the houses and the accompanying landscape continued to follow British design ideas, since although they had won the war the newly independent Americans held no durable animosity toward their former masters. Pieces of graceful statuary wrought from stone or metal were introduced as decorative garden ornaments along with shaded arbors and teahouses. Outdoor socializing became an important activity in all major cities, and garden layouts of more complex interest naturally followed suit.

At the beginning of the nineteenth century both nurseries and seed com-

A replica of an eighteenth-century wood fence, Williamsburg, Virginia.

panies in the United States logically promoted a wealth of new plant types from Europe. For the larger households, employing a staff of skilled caretakers became a necessity for managing the now-enlarged grounds. This expanded interest in horticultural improvement led to the related creation of organized garden centers, which soon became commonplace. The march of the American public toward a "bigger, better, and brighter" plant world had begun.

Residential landscape design in the United States from 1841 onward was enduringly influenced by the publication in New York of architect and nurseryman Andrew Jackson Downing's illustrated book on creating rural landscape art: *Treatise on the Theory and Practice of Landscape Gardening.* Downing established that correct elegance came only from a tasteful layout represented in a naturalistic style, and naturalism was, therefore, the hallmark of the best designs. He curiously avoided designing any of his clients' houses in the standard classical form and favored, instead, the Tudor, Gothic, and Renaissance revivals, with their ascending peaks and turrets, because to him these appealing building

An early-nineteenth-century stone garden statue in Massachusetts.

A replica of an early-nineteenth-century teahouse, Massachusetts.

elements more closely imitated the mountains and treetops of the desirable rustic Nature.

Downing stressed to his enthusiastic public that the lay of the existing land should automatically dictate the ultimate plan for all home grounds. His dictum allowed rock ledge to remain exposed, valley depressions to be left unfilled, and existing vegetation to grow untouched except for absolutely essential removals. He further scorned all foundation planting around a house (obviously he admired the earlier theories of Brown and Repton in Great Britain), except for plants set into the open lawn facing the residence, which he coined "carpet bedding." Such bedding-out meant installing one or more large, circular displays of bright and especially fragrant summer annuals to be enjoyed both from the open windows of the house as well as by approaching visitors. Essential vegetable plots and fruit orchards on the property were masked from view by vine-covered trellises at the rear or side of the lot. Surprisingly influential, Downing's design book held continual popularity in the United States and Europe through ten printings right into the twentieth century.

The chief American proponent of the pastoral landscape treatment for public grounds was Frederick Law Olmsted, whose huge development for Central Park in New York City during the 1850s became the most imitated model for naturalistic parks in major American cities. A champion of utility and serving the plain necessities of human living, Olmsted also explored at great length how to improve residential subdivisions. He strongly urged the inclusion of gracefully curved streets, with individual homes set far back from the street, generous street-tree plantings throughout, and unifying ribbons of paved sidewalks to connect neighbors in a more closely knit community. He further promoted leaving sizable natural stands of woodlot available for continued appreciation of Nature's original bounty. With Olmsted all development sites for houselots required careful and thorough investigation, not quick obliteration for commercial convenience by the builders. His astute planning conceptions received national praise and endorsement all through the nineteenth century's last decades, and today Olmsted is commonly recognized as the founding father of landscape architecture in America. From the Atlantic to the Pacific, his design activity left a permanent mark still cherished today by anyone who appreciates the value of our outdoor environment.

During the middle and late Victorian era from 1850 to 1900, Downing's garden ideas carried even greater prominence, but unfortunately his original flower-bedding commandment became increasingly complex in form and detailing. Every urban and suburban household with any amount of land seemed bent on outdoing its neighbor not only with elaborate lawn displays of colorful plants but also with statuary pieces and other noticeable artifacts. This constant occupation with intricate detailing for all outdoor surfaces also expanded into ornately scrolled house trim painted in a remarkable variety of colorations. Elaborately embellished metal fencing became the norm on every street, while in private garden spaces overly convoluted garden seating surely made women glad they had a bustle on which to rest. Simplicity of any sort virtually disappeared under a staggering load of overlay decoration.

An elaborate Victorian-style arrangement of summer annuals, Italy.

Garden form and design identification now sank into chaos, and for a brief time fashion even dictated that a variety of landscape styles could be set cheek to jowl on a single property. It was possible to find not only an Italian garden and a rustic woodland shelter but also a German grotto and a French parterre entangled together in one crowded space. This overly ornamented period concluded by the early 1900s with unfocused clutter as its historic legacy.

By the early part of the twentieth century a logical movement away from the fifty years of increasingly stuffy Victorian values became evident in many ways. Architecture, clothing styles, social habits, and garden design at last headed in a refreshing direction that stressed more straightforward and open-minded public attitudes. All art forms benefited by the rise of the Arts and Crafts Movement, where admiration for the basic nature of all materials led to the rediscovered pleasure of simplified expressions. In horticulture the cottage garden gained popularity with its tangled but friendly masses of unfettered annuals, perennials, roses, and herbs, while the long, lush perennial borders for country houses, promoted so enthusiastically by the British gardener Gertrude Jekyll, won enduring support and repeated imitation in the United States.

Other vital design influences were also at work in architecture, painting, and sculpture. European Modernism of the 1920s broke new ground by loud-

Fern-patterned metal chairs from the late-Victorian era.

ly trumpeting the unique value of integrating indoor and outdoor spaces with glass walls and crisper garden layouts. Cubism in painting was echoed by similarly abstract landscape forms that featured massed, single-species beds of bright flowers or colored-foliage ground covers in boxy but simple presentations. These bold plantings often surrounded a contemporary sculpture or fountain of unusual configuration and size that would have completely baffled—and shocked—a Victorian audience.

Curiously, this was also a time of sizable "country places" both in America and abroad, which saw a nostalgic revival of the older garden styles accompanying the many replicas of homes from far-away periods. Gothic, Tudor, Renaissance, and Georgian house reproductions again took hold of the public's imagination, and these styles were strongly reinforced throughout the 1920s. Of course, wealth in this period was abundant, taxes were ridiculously low, good help was plentiful, and a mood of security and social tranquillity abounded. All these interwoven factors readily supported the widespread demand for estate

A modern bedding design of begonias, Italy.

building on an elaborate scale. The labor-intensive and expensive home and garden efforts quickly faded, however, with the worldwide Great Depression of the 1930s and did not find comparable renewal until after World War II.

By the 1950s substantial improvements in the technical means for doing work more efficiently with less cost contributed markedly to an increased emphasis on functionalism throughout the design professions. Designers stressed that all elements of a site should logically reflect the orderliness of a spatial master plan that smoothly blended each part into an appealing, utilitarian whole. The French-Swiss architect Le Corbusier had decreed in the 1930s that the house was a "machine for living in," with its newly streamlined silhouette, convivial open spaces inside and out, plus its many labor-saving devices. California de-

A 1920s "country place" estate in Long Island, New York.

signers soon after championed extended outdoor living, which created wide-spread public enthusiasm and the start of a keener appreciation of more natu-ralistic garden landscapes from coast to coast.

Lower maintenance, more reliable and carefree plant material, coupled with an extravaganza of time-saving garden equipment—and more environmentally responsible landscape designs—are all part of today's garden atmosphere. Be-cause knowledgeable gardening help is now difficult to find—and pay for—we have largely adjusted to "do-it-yourself" programs with only occasional out-side assistance. Even though it is said that "time began in a garden," we are learn-ing nowadays that time is a precious commodity few have in useful abundance. Still, garden-making efforts are continually on the rise throughout the world, and that news should reassure us that it is still a human delight to be surrounded by thriving vegetation and appropriate artifacts no matter how we decide to arrange them for eye-appealing satisfaction. In sum, a garden has yesterday, today, and tomorrow firmly interwoven into our lives.

A contemporary fenced garden in Massachusetts.

Chapter 2

Basic Agenda
for Evaluating Your Site

Any decision about making a change to your home grounds naturally has to begin with an analysis of what you already have. Then you need a clear understanding of your intended goals and how you plan to arrive at a satisfactory resolution for those aims. This chapter presents some initial site considerations to help in your evaluation.

Outlining Your Goals

Site alterations are always tied to your own reactions to what you believe needs adjustment for greater personal enjoyment. Since no two properties are ever fully identical, and no two houses are exact twins or situated precisely alike, you can expect that no two garden treatments will ever be duplicates either. We all have different garden interpretations in mind, and if you absorb the highlights of design recommendations presented throughout this book, you should be well on your way to creating your own individualistic setting. Just remember that garden design is not mere decoration but a genuine effort at problem solving in a practical and durable—as well as attractive—way.

Before you can move securely into actual revamping of an area, however, you should raise some pertinent questions about what goals you hope to accomplish as well as your priorities for fulfilling them. Should you start with privacy screening? Do you require a safe, grassy space for frolicking children or romping pets? Where will you place the children's play equipment? Can you

44

profit from a better-organized area for various types of outdoor socializing? Is a swimming pool essential to your fitness or fun routine? Would you enjoy a cozy outdoor retreat, perhaps with a shelter, that comfortably secludes you from distractions? Is raising vegetables or fruit of interest to you? Are there convenient spaces for equipment storage and outdoor work areas? Are you keen to establish some showcase plant collection? What is your list of "must-have" plant materials? Does your existing planting need enhancing, transplanting, or discarding? Will maintenance requirements necessitate alternatives to existing plants or construction materials?

These are just a few of the many motivations for change, so jot down all the garden requirements you find compelling, along with their rank of importance. You may end up with a long list or a short one, but in either case you will have supplied yourself with a usefully clarified focus. Of course, it would be delightful if your budget, energy, and time frame could easily allow all your

An organized space for outdoor socializing is always a welcome addition to a site.

This shelter and grape arbor provide a secluded hideaway for private contemplation on Nantucket Island, Massachusetts.

An extravaganza of spring bulbs glows with showcase appeal.

landscape wishes to become reality tomorrow, but that joy is not commonplace. Most of us have to be practical and postpone parts of the plan a bit longer. Such delay is no real handicap since it provides additional time to mull over priorities, and surprisingly some ideas do get adjusted—or even eliminated—as time goes by. This is only natural as we go about using our grounds.

In any event, once you establish your needs and priorities in a clear and workable fashion you are ready to move on to the many details necessary for a unified and satisfying outcome. Each of the various site considerations explained here and elsewhere in the book is independently relevant for making intelligent decisions, but taken together they form a cohesive framework. Your first step is simply to review the possibilities and pitfalls of both the site and your intended program with a critical eye. While each garden space can be a unique canvas for personal expression, some land areas are better than others as far as usefulness and convenience, and you need to determine how these concerns relate on your own grounds.

Open Space

Keep in mind that available outdoor space on a houselot is not only determined by the size, shape, and contours of your parcel but also by the location and volume of the house itself. All tall objects cast significant shadows that affect parts of every site during each season, and a house normally casts the largest and most solid one. The orientation of the building determines where its longest shadow will fall. A north-facing structure, for example, will have a frontage that is dimly lit while the rear will likely be basking in full brightness. Of course, any tall trees surrounding the rear of the lot can diminish the area in sun there, too, and a mass of evergreen trees will bring deep shading all year long. If you require maximum sunshine over the area, then you will have to consider some tree removals.

Land that is steeply sloped or has large, exposed boulders or rock outcrops offers additional challenges for the simple development of any spaces for recreational or gardening uses. Natural wetlands on the property also can present difficulties for further development, particularly since most communities nowadays observe restrictive wetland ordinances. Then the existing plantings must be evaluated by type, size, condition, and distribution over the entire area, along with the future value to your garden intentions, whether left in place or transplanted elsewhere on the site. Not every existing plant has to be cherished, of course, but if you are unclear about the merits of any, you should pay for a plant specialist to visit and identify the worth before you start any remodeling. If you see a need to remove quantities of trees or boulders, then consider this messy work a first priority.

Three main plant types make up the natural vegetation cover, and together they form outdoor enclosures similar to an interior room. The tree canopy is the ceiling, understory shrubs translate into walls, and lawn and ground cover plants logically form the flooring. Outdoor space, of course, is normally far greater in volume than any found indoors, and because plants expand yearly,

Natural and introduced vegetation form the ceiling, walls, and flooring of enclosed outdoor spaces.

you should think through first how future growth of both existing and new plantings will affect your development scheme.

Soil Composition

Because soil is the basic medium for growing plants, you should determine early on its depth and composition at all parts of the site. Soils not only vary throughout every community but often change radically even on the same property. No garden soil is just one common mix of ingredients but is normally a conglomeration of organic matter, sand, silt, clay, and different-sized stones in varying proportions from one location to another. Nevertheless, soil composition is a vitally important aspect of a site to understand since it determines how much rainfall will be readily absorbed and how much will remain available for plant roots during the growing season. The soil type—acid or alkaline—further establishes which plants will adapt easily and thrive. For example, azaleas and rhododendrons are intolerant of highly alkaline soils altogether, while osmanthus and Darwin's barberry (*Berberis darwinii*) are sickly in acid ones. Curiously, the majority of junipers are content either way. As you undoubtedly already know, sandy soil drains rapidly but clay-laced soil drains sluggishly.

Of course, there are a wide variety of soil mixes throughout the world and plant types adapted best for each of them. Find out the general structure of your soil simply by digging a modest-sized hole up to 18 inches deep in a root-free area and inspect the excavated material. Make several of these test holes throughout the property to verify any variations that may exist. You may be surprised at the results, but this basic soil knowledge will prove very helpful to your horticultural success.

In this dug earth, topsoil is the darker, crumbly, uppermost layer and represents decayed organic matter, which contains most of the nutrients needed for suitable plant growth. Its depth is highly variable on most sites. Subsoil is directly beneath it and varies in color, texture, and depth. This layer often contains some pebbles or large stones—and perhaps even discarded construction materials near the walls of the buildings—and has less nutrient value than topsoil. Clay hardpan may appear on some sites below the subsoil and is sticky, constantly moist, and very dense. Hardpan does not drain well at all, and plant roots usually ride atop this clay, creating somewhat insecure anchoring. Planting on raised beds is one solution to the problem if the result can be arranged to appear natural with the adjacent grading.

If you have any serious doubts about your soil's current quality, you should have samples tested for composition and nutrient value either by a state-run, co-operative field station nearby or else by a commercial soil-testing laboratory. After you read the report and learn of any important soil deficiencies, you can either make these soil improvements yourself or hire a local contractor to pro-vide the materials and labor necessary to upgrade the situation. Be aware, how-ever, that this remedial action is not always a one-time operation since contin-ued plant growth can deplete these soil modifications in a short time.

Surface-Water Drainage

Proper surface-water flow will always help you to obtain the best landscape set-ting and planting response. Gravity dictates that rainfall moves from any high

This railroad-tie wall effectively redirects surface-water runoff away from the house foun-dation and adjoining terrace.

point toward a lower one, but this simple movement can also cause excess water to accumulate elsewhere on your land and create further problems. When rain or melting snow fail to move quickly from any area, the resultant puddling can become a handicap to both people and plants. Minor earth grading (see also Chapter 3) by filling small, low areas with more soil is an obvious solution, of course, but with significant and lasting water collection you may have to install subsurface drain lines and surface pick-ups (grated inlets or catch basins) instead. Water standing for long periods also creates oxygen-depleted soil and contributes to greater compaction, which few plants readily tolerate.

Steep embankments near essential use areas of a home may even need masonry or wood-tie retaining walls (see also Chapter 3) to flatten some portions of the existing grading as well as to slow down or redirect the wash of rain water coming from above. Repeated soil erosion and flooding are not minor matters on any site and will continue until properly corrected. Once again, ascertain whether surface-water runoff is a potential handicap on any part of the intended development well before you start any site remodeling.

Factors of Sun, Shade, Wind, and Dryness

The amount of sunshine, shade, and wind affecting a site, especially during the seasonal high-use times, will be important influences on your basic design ideas and require careful evaluation. An area that receives full sun at least eight hours daily in summertime provides the greatest design versatility from a long list of plant choices and is considered ideal for a sturdy turf suitable both for play areas and entertaining on a large scale.

Semishaded spaces of appreciable size reduce the potential planting list as well as the vigor of lawn, while dense shading further curtails them both. Constant dimness from the solid shadows of tall buildings, high walls or fences, and sizable evergreens also keeps the soil cooler much longer and often contributes to later blooming times for flowering plants. Every garden has shading to some degree, of course, and it can be a welcome asset to be enjoyed or an annoying handicap to be overcome, depending upon your attitude toward it. On your own land it is a personally manageable situation, but if the shading comes from a neighbor's construction or planting efforts, you have little recourse but to accept its presence.

Windiness on a site also has its benefits and its drawbacks. A consistently pleasant summer breeze will make any garden area more inviting and promote healthier plant response, but strong or drying (or icy) winds often prove uncomfortable and may even stunt normal plant expansion and flowering. Windscreens composed from tolerant planting, sturdy fencing, or masonry walls can rectify the situation satisfactorily, yet such structures may also introduce significant shade, thereby potentially exchanging one problem for another.

Dryness is another part of the existing conditions that must be understood. Large, established trees and shrubs of every sort have thirsty roots widely fanning out in every direction that naturally deplete the organic material and draw available moisture consistently from the surrounding soil. Such congested root

Located in full sun, this generous area of sturdy grass turf is useful for both play and socializing.

masses make it difficult to introduce any new planting successfully within their spreads unless it is highly drought-tolerant material. Even lawn grass has a problem enduring attractively with such root and sunlight competition, although substitute ground covers, such as English ivy (*Hedera*) or periwinkle (*Vinca*), often tolerate these troublesome growing conditions.

The existing plantings, earth contours, soil composition, surface-water drainage, and degree of sun, shade, wind, and dryness are the major conditions to evaluate, then, before you launch into the specific design changes for a site's personalized development. A clear understanding of these factors will help greatly toward achieving success more easily.

Chapter 3

Major Components of Garden Design

Once you have thoroughly investigated and evaluated the existing conditions of your site, you next should become involved with those special design ingredients that will be essential to your composition. These include your chosen style of the creation, the inclusion of suitable construction and artifacts, the proper color harmonies, and the form, texture, and size of the various items placed in association with one another. Some earth moving may be necessary as well to provide usable platforms for the intended program or to make improvements in drainage flow. The first consideration, the overall style, is the detailed statement of a particular way of living by means of the layout and components of the grounds. Today we are presented with three main categories for personal expression: formal, informal, and to a lesser degree, naturalized.

Formal or Symmetric Details

Formal style, also known as symmetric, is the most architectural in appearance, producing a well-liked, orderly, and calming effectiveness. This approach can be reflected in either a straight-line or geometrically curved layout and seeks to balance identical planting and construction elements equally on both sides of a central axis. The axis often terminates at one special focal point, usually the main entry of a house but it can also end at a statue, a garden fountain, a teahouse, or any other major object.

Though perfectly flat terrain is not essential for a fulfilling and visually suitable formal design, the main component of such a space is far more effective when established on a flattish piece of ground. With this treatment, the unique layout can be viewed either from the main windows of a house or from an adjacent raised terrace or porch, providing a compelling display of its artistic merits. Historically such crisp garden design patterning agreeably belongs with the architectural styles found in many older house configurations that clearly exhibit a noteworthy balance of the various building parts. Yet, a formal design can be appropriate for an offset or subsidiary garden space at a contemporary residence when modified by minimizing the area the garden occupies, by simplifying the construction detailing, and by reducing the color range and variety of plants used. Formality is not tied to the size of the project but to the partic-

This sizable, formal layout of summer annuals in Rhode Island befits the house's large size and formal architectural style.

ular handling of all its components. In brief, treat formalism loosely in certain circumstances as an exercise for visual surprise engendered by personalized wit. Formalism should not necessarily translate to stuffiness.

Symmetric balance in a formalized garden design is ideally expressed by a series of equally matched beds—either square, rectangular, curved, or a hybrid of all three—with identically sized walks threading through the layout, perhaps bordered crisply by cut stone or brick curbing. These bedding outlines might be further emphasized by the addition of low, clipped hedges—preferably evergreen for year-round interest—between level paths covered either with grass turf or neatly laid paving of brick, flat stone of uniform color, compacted gravel, or small, loose stones. As you can undoubtedly tell from these specifics, formal layouts normally rely as much on precise architectural detailing as on the planting choices.

Some formal garden spaces are enclosed on three sides by a sheared hedge

A smaller, contemporary interpretation of a formal bed using annuals in Massachusetts.

of tall, evergreen or close-twigged deciduous plants for a solid-looking enframement of the attractions laid out within the area. Other enclosure treatments include a hefty masonry wall of neatly fitted stone or uniform brick, perhaps partially covered by choice vines. The fourth, viewing end of an enclosure can either be left entirely unobstructed or bordered by a hedge or wall shorter than the other sections. Another variation on the rear wall enclosure is to include an open balustrade or other opening for glimpsing an enticing landscape scene that lies just beyond. To achieve more uniform growth response for an enclosing hedge line, orient the main axis of the garden on a north-south basis, which provides more equalized sunlight than an east-west orientation does.

Elevated interest and intricacy within a formal garden can be supplied by large, matched urns—either solid, carved forms or open bowl types lushly filled with plants—placed on pedestals. Thematically related statuary of appropriate scale, topiary trees or shrubs, and neatly shaped climbing roses or clematis, sup-

The matched raised beds, brick curbing, and brick-paved walks on this Texas site create a symmetric balance.

ported by sturdy yet decorative wood or metal structures, are other attractive details. Be sure that all such artifacts are weatherproofed for your climate, or else you will be hauling them back and forth each season, a chore no one enjoys.

Maintenance costs, unfortunately, are always high with formal garden layouts since every plant must receive perfect grooming at all times, and the construction elements must be kept in excellent repair. Such a workload will undoubtedly require some outside assistance, especially during the growing season, if these special displays are extensive. Obviously, this gardening technique is not suited to a thin pocketbook or wallet if it is to look its best continually, yet it offers a dramatic gardening treatment with long-lasting appeal and charm to which many subscribers are addicted.

Noticeable topiary forms dominate this portion of a formal layout in California.

Informal or Asymmetric Details

Informal balance is also known as asymmetry, and the many evident examples clearly establish it as the most popular garden style today. Here the design arrangement is directed toward a mostly nonrepetitive grouping of plant material, which conveys a more relaxed, interwoven presentation, yet the entire composition must still show a visually comfortable balance in its masses, textures, dimensions, and colorings throughout. Introduced structures and ornamental accents such as a paved terrace or wood deck, a fountain or waterfall, a birdbath or statue, and even a swimming pool can be free-flowing in appearance, but each item must contribute a full measure of harmony and proper scale to the entire scene. Freedom of expression is still guided by rules.

In a way, using informal design in a garden is a bit more complex than the formal mode, for while you have greater flexibility, you also have fewer directions to lead you along the way to satisfying fulfillment. Informal layouts, nev-

This asymmetric planting of drought-tolerant material in Arizona offers a lush effect.

ertheless, often lead to greater experimentation, and that aspect is surely what makes the style so appealing to a consistently broad audience.

Informality offers the potential for creating seasonal garden interest even in a small area without nearly the effort involved with formal statements. Collections of spring bulbs, together with early blooming shrubs and perennials, in one part of the garden can be supplanted later in another section by a different focus—even entirely different colorings—such as summer bulbs, late-blooming shrubs, and vibrant annuals. I follow that seasonal routine every year in my own garden and enjoy the shift of spatial emphasis.

When creating these variable-season color allotments, be sure to avoid a "polka dot" look by not planting one of every intriguing item that caught your fancy. This splintered appearance could make it seem like you bought out a nursery. Instead, for a stronger visual effect install sizable groups of the same plant, especially with bulbs, perennials, and annuals. Keep in mind that horticulture is growing plants well but design is arranging them well. All aspects of your garden development should importantly involve both considerations with equal enthusiasm.

Pruning requirements are less demanding with informal layouts since here you are shaping plant outlines toward graceful natural forms with only modest control. Sadly, far too many homeowners annually butcher their expanding trees and shrubs (or pay someone else to commit the crime) into blobs of totally incongruous silhouettes to keep the plants at so-called manageable size. What a waste of time and energy! Such consistent shearing introduces formal topiary shapes where they do not rightly belong, but the truth is such plant choices were incorrect in the first place if they need such drastic handling. Be wise and learn beforehand what size each plant will normally reach in your area before you, too, have to grab the clippers. There are always great numbers of available plant choices that easily keep their mature dimensions in bounds, but you have to want to learn this valuable information.

Naturalized or Rustic Details

The naturalized style of gardening—sometimes labeled rustic—takes the informal approach a giant step backward. Its main principle seems to focus on accepting as satisfactory every detail that Nature puts before us, encouraging few, if any, changes to established plantings, earth contours, water features, or exposed boulders. (The premise closely aligns with what Alexander Jackson Downing promoted during the mid-1800s, as reported in Chapter 1.) Native trees, shrubs, vines, ferns, and wildflowers are allowed to "do their own thing" without human interference.

In this style, regularly mowed lawn for play or entertaining is normally kept to a minimum and may even be bordered by banks of rampant weeds and fully grown grasses. Introduced necessities such as paths, steps, fences, and seats fit such a scheme best if left primitively simple throughout. Nevertheless, this system has merit since it is nicely adaptable for some vacation and woodlot homes for those with a "less work is best" attitude toward gardening. Not everyone needs to conform to over-managing the plant world, and that is hardly a fault warranting undue criticism.

Naturalized or rustic spaces do not involve much maintenance but still create visual interest.

Just the same, a determined few homeowners attempt to bring untamed Nature back into the city by neglecting their own grassy areas entirely or by converting frontage turf into free-seeding wildflower extravaganzas that send their productivity far and wide. Handsome as some of these experiments may be, they can create neighborhood problems. Of course, there are also well-managed wildflower plots in the city and in suburbia that merit applause for their true beauty and interest, but that is not the same as the enthusiast for naturalism who appears unbothered by wildly overgrown shrubs and myriad tree seedlings crowding every inch of the land not covered by straggly weeds. Use care when introducing this laid-back gardening technique beyond its usual countryside boundaries.

Earth Grading

Just about every garden development at some point needs a site adjustment that involves earth modeling. Grading the land is most often concerned with creating a different-size or different-level space for greater usefulness, such as flattening the land for a recreational playfield or a swimming pool, but it also can be employed to adjust surface-water drainage flow or to create additional parking. Additionally, newly constructed walls of stone, brick, cement concrete, or wood ties may be necessary to support the restructured contours and prevent erosion (see also the section on "Walls" later in this chapter).

Although many grading problems can be readily rectified with just hand labor, more often than not significant changes will require that you bring in a bulldozer or backhoe for greater efficiency and a quicker timetable for completion. Heavy-duty equipment is a high expense, especially the flatbed truck to haul the equipment, and it is more economical to schedule all necessary grading at one time rather than doling it out to fit a particular budget.

When you are lucky, the cut-from-here and fill-over-there procedure of grading can work satisfactorily with soil already on the property. If it does not work out that way, you will have to buy, haul, and spread additional soil (possibly subsoil as well as topsoil) to complete the work. Be certain that the new earth supply is the same quality as, if not better than, the existing soil, and be wary of a gift conveniently available at low cost since it may later prove to be "junk" with negative results for plant growth. To be safe, ask for a soil sample to inspect and approve before any deliveries are made.

With every machine-oriented grading operation, all existing trees and shrubs to be left undisturbed in the work area should be well protected from stem damage or root compaction by the equipment through the use of sturdy barrier fencing set as far away as possible from the plants. Avoid smothering trunks and roots with deep piles of fill material since stems and roots are plant-breathing areas as much as leaves are. Another point to keep in mind is to wait for good weather before moving soil because muddy or frozen soil will not knit together satisfactorily and will be riddled with air pockets, which is not ideal for later root response.

Stone walls support the revised grading at this redesigned entry garden.

Water Features

No design element brings greater interest and sustained pleasure to a landscape scene than a water feature. Whether still or moving, water consistently supplies us with welcome and soothing effects of sight, sound, and perhaps touch for our delight. The sound of gushing water seems to act as a magnet drawing people to investigate its location. Because water also remains a continuing life force for both people and plants at all times, its inclusion into our garden planning is relevant for even the smallest space.

A body of still water, whether natural or artificial, contributes placid simplicity to a landscape view (and may even attract wildlife if it is large enough), and actively moving water offers addictive stimulation to ear and eye from its sounds and changing patterns. With either choice, a water feature should intelligently fit the scale of its surroundings and be totally sympathetic in its style,

This large artificial pond quickly drew an appreciative wildlife population.

coloring, and construction materials with adjoining garden treatments. Water features also provide a way to introduce new or unusual plant materials, such as by using sunken tubs of water lilies and clumps of papyrus as part of a shallow still-water basin or by installing marsh marigolds, primroses, and ostrich ferns, for example, in the boggy soils surrounding a natural or created pond. Water gardening opens new avenues of design interest wherever it is utilized.

A birdbath, reflecting pool, fountain, and waterfall are all age-old embellishments for countless gardens around the world not only because people consistently enjoy them, but also because such water features are useful for many of the daily routines of wildlife. Chittering birds flitting in and out of a decorative garden basin provide color, movement, and splash noises with their agitated bathing routines. (Be sure to include some tall, twiggy plants close at hand to protect the birds from predators as well as to offer convenient waiting areas for the next in line.) Large sheets of mirroring water even of shallow depth reflect sky views and other surrounding objects, while providing nesting and paddling spaces for various water fowl in natural settings. A fountain with a simple or elaborate spout of high-stretching water catches the glint of sunlight, spreads coolness to its surroundings (plus occasional wind-driven spray, too), and punctuates the air with rhythmic sounds we enjoy hearing repeated. A waterfall or cascade of even modest size and flow can readily mask the sounds of noisy distractions beyond the garden borders. Water in the landscape plays many roles in giving us pleasure.

Normally built to suit a particular site when designed as a sizable feature, a garden fountain can be arranged with its rim either at ground level or raised conspicuously above. An aboveground basin is often constructed in place with cement concrete topped with a well-scaled coping of stone, brick, or tile, yet showrooms and catalogs are filled with precast or artisan-carved models, too. The receiving basin, of course, should be wide enough to contain all the returning droplets neatly, especially if the jet reach is high or the location is prone to sudden wind gusts. Both a clean-out drain and an overflow pipe are useful inclusions.

A fountain feature of good size usually has its water supply piped to the unit on its own line, and the electric-operated submersible pump and filter activating the flow can be set into a small reservoir chamber beneath the main jet or even placed outside the basin. Fountain action begins by throwing a toggle switch conveniently located within the house, while the display is controlled mainly by a series of fountainheads and the number of spray holes in each head. Be aware, however, that tiny openings clog easily from all sorts of airborne debris, which only a forceful surge of start-up water can dislodge easily.

A contemporary interpretation, especially useful for small spaces, is a drip fountain, with its different water levels and varying sizes of tilted, open bowls or troughs arranged along a rigid vertical support. Whether factory-produced or handcrafted, this fountain style pumps water from the lowest and largest basin at ground level up through a central supply pipe (which is just a garden hose standing stiffly at attention) either to bubble down from the top or else strike a restraining hood before its descent. The effect is both subtle as well as quietly soothing for a private sitting or eating area. The sculptural fountainworks, of

Water sparkles attractively from this sizable fountain feature.

course, is pleasantly on view at all times. This is one of the easiest water features to install and maintain.

While a birdbath and fountain are generally recognized as artificial sources of outdoor water, a waterfall can be made to appear naturalistic when built directly into a substantial rise of a landscape background. Because the affiliation of rocks and running water in Nature is commonplace, we often bring them together in some fashion for gardens as well. Boulders artfully set not only can disguise the construction parts of this feature (mainly cement concrete basins and water travelways) but also can interrupt or redirect the flow through the sluice channel. The greater volume of falling water from a waterfall or wall-mounted cascade has the potential to mask other nearby sounds when the height and gallonage are maximized. Of course, a waterfall need not always be noisy for garden effectiveness and can also be arranged just to trickle sedately and thread its way down through a hillside rock garden to an awaiting basin.

The key to visual suitability is to have the waterfall always positioned to flow logically from a high elevation, whether this grade exists naturally or has to

A drip fountain contributes a consistent sculptural form to the garden.

be created. Waterfalls recirculate their contents just as a fountain does, but now you need two basins: one at the top to produce the proper volume and another at the bottom containing the pump to recirculate the water to the top. A high level of evaporation will usually result from this vigorous action, especially on very warm and windy days, so both basins may need frequent replenishing, either manually by a hose or with a supply valve that will open when the water level reaches a preset low point in the pump basin.

Simple water features can be successfully installed as do-it-yourself projects. After all, a birdbath can be hauled into place without the need for special assistance. Nevertheless, before tackling any complicated water feature, you will do well to consult with a known expert in the field for guidance. Beyond understanding the basic requirements for durable water-basin construction, plus the correct method for installing piping, pumps, filters, overflow pipes, clean-out drains, and an electrical supply, you should also focus on creating a healthy

This compelling garden waterfall and lily pool in Montreal reflect a common scene from Nature.

water system. Whether for use by fish, plants, or people, the water must be safe and attractively presented on a daily basis. This entails practical maintenance, the frequency of which will vary with the usage and size of the feature. Be certain you fully understand all the necessary rules before you authorize construction. Consulting early with a water specialist helps greatly in avoiding future problems and extra maintenance.

Although natural water flowing into or through your property can be a wonderfully attractive and desirable addition to the setting, you will experience far different circumstances in handling its arrangement, seasonal volume, and on-site function compared to created water features. Rarely will you be able to fully control the source or run of a stream, which can often overflow its banks and cause flooding in any season, depending upon your geographic location. Of course, this same channel can just as easily diminish to an inconsequential trickle during dry times. You might try damming to create a broad retention pond,

Here a trickling hillside waterfall is framed by dwarf conifers and heather.

but this simple solution may lead to conflicts if this same water volume also serves downstream abutters who would naturally expect the same flow they saw last week. At least with any artificial water features you can better manage its use.

An in-ground swimming pool will most likely be the largest water feature on any property, and it is a social magnet with great appeal, especially in areas where its merits for health and play can be enjoyed for most of the year. Potentially a pool complex has four main components: the pool itself, the surrounding pavement or wood decking, a storage building to house the pool equipment, and finally, a required security fence. As you might expect, each element of this large-scale project is more difficult to blend into adjacent surroundings, but since a pool is a permanent investment of considerable cost and continual upkeep, you should carefully evaluate its many details from the start.

For improved convenience and attractiveness throughout its season of use, a pool should be located close to the main access from the house and, of course, adequately set back from property lines in compliance with local ordinances. Keep in mind that the off-season safety cover might become visually intrusive for months on end and should thus be masked from view with adequate planting. Make certain your chosen site receives the maximum daily sunshine during high-use times, particularly that portion allocated as the lounging area. Position the pool as far away as possible from the falling debris of deciduous trees as well as from the dense spring pollen drop of pines or the messy fruit splatter of certain palms, for example. This guideline will keep both you and your pool filter from running overtime with constant clean-up.

A full-sized swimming pool (or a narrow lap version) often plays two roles during the course of a day, becoming an ornamental body of water when not in active use. The contribution as a special garden feature in evening and nighttime can be greatly enhanced when lit by the soft glow of one or two submerged lamps set into the basin construction. This subtle lighting not only adds a useful element of safety but encourages socializing around its perimeter. Muted lighting is also far more neighborly—and less bug attracting—than dazzling cones of area illumination hung from elevated poles.

The size of a pool is a variable determined not only by the available land area, and your budget allowance, but also by the final proportions most appropriate for pleasurable use. A basic guideline is to have the length at least twice the width. When deciding upon a shape you will find that formalized, rectilinear designs also promote similarly neat, geometric forms in the adjacent pavement or deckwork. Informal layouts, on the other hand, allow for a wide variety of sinuous pool shapes, surrounding pavement, and planting additions. Your own lifestyle will direct you to the better choice here.

Either smooth pavement or wood decking should enclose all edges of the pool to allow necessary maintenance access to every part. Choose a material with low glare that is compatible with the rest of the setting. Slope all paving modestly away from the pool edge to direct surface water toward nearby planting beds or else into an existing or added storm drain system. Always avoid installing grass lawn close to the pool to prevent mowed clippings from regularly blowing into the water. Mower bags also help greatly on any lawn space since

At this formal setting in eastern New York State, the swimming pool is successfully blended into the composition.

they collect cut grass before it is tracked into the pool. Under no circumstances should you include turf grass between any decking stones since proper maintenance is far too time-consuming to be worthwhile. These grassy strips also create stumbling points in a short time.

Although the equipment required for the proper functioning and upkeep of a pool can be positioned inside the house on some sites, you will undoubtedly find it more sensible to erect a conveniently located, independent storage building for housing the filtering machinery, other pool necessities, and off-season furniture. This basic structure can be enlarged to accommodate a changing room, an outside shower area, and a wind-protected withdrawal space. If your social activity does demand these larger proportions, your pool house can become an imposing addition in the landscape. It will require more attention about its height and volume, its construction detailing, and the choice of building material, plus, of course, its correct positioning to fit comfortably and not overwhelm the site.

By law a swimming pool, legally defined as an "attractive nuisance," must have a security fence completely surrounding its area. Required fencing heights

Informality abounds at this salt-water pool and rustic shelter of coastal Maine.

vary by community, yet the choice of the fencing material itself is normally left to the owner as long as it is durable and sturdy enough to resist easy intrusion. Of course, masonry walls and solid wood fencing provide the most privacy—but also less cross ventilation—and most people opt for a mesh-wire fencing if the site conditions are favorable to openness, particularly if an attractive view is gained. For inconspicuousness choose a 2-inch, chain-link fence precoated with black or dark brown vinyl for long-lasting durability. (The omnipresent green finish promoted today is far more noticeable than either of these dark colors and never matches any nearby plant foliage satisfactorily.) Keep in mind that the location of this fencing does not have to be immediately adjacent to the pool but can be hidden farther away—even out to your property line—as long as it creates a uniform enclosure. The pool house can also act as part of the barrier.

Any close-by fencing should be softened in appearance either with flowering, scented vines or adjacent shrub and flower beds, preferably those with well-mannered blossoming and fruiting habits. Seasonal annuals in large, decorative, and preferably weatherproof pots or tubs can contribute significant color as well. When handled attractively in all its parts, a swimming pool can be a

Black-vinyl-coated chain-link fencing around a pool serves its safety function unobtrusively.

significant "outdoor room" on a property (see the section "Outdoor Rooms" in this chapter).

Another technique, the so-called horse fence, may at first seem nonconforming in its openness but actually provides both safe enclosure and useful distant views from the pool. A neat line of three equally spaced, horizontal wood rails, backed completely with an almost-invisible, one-inch mesh of vinyl-coated wire stapled directly to the poolside sections of the wood, can be an effective resolution to fencing needs. Keeping all planting additions outside the pool enclosure allows for greater freedom of expression in the planting design. There is always a new way to resolve a familiar problem when you put your mind to it.

Walls

A substantial outdoor enclosure is recognized everywhere as the traditional symbol for defining a private garden space, whether it is made by a wall, a fence, or a hedge (see Chapter 9 for plant details). Any wall conveys a comforting recognition of reliable permanence from the solid materials used, such as brick or stone, arranged either to be a free-standing barrier or a retaining device built into the earth to support grade changes. Even though both wall types are always expensive to construct in time and materials, each can readily be adjusted to fit a particular site, garden style, or budget with proper planning. Some garden situations require finely made detailing, of course, but out-of-the-way areas can show less fussiness and still be visually pleasant as well as practical.

Any wall, however, should be treated as an architectural statement so that both the top and sides are always kept level and plumb to the eye, just as you would expect to find in a well-constructed building. Granted, there is a wall-building technique that uses a battered front, which slopes the face back by roughly an inch for every foot of rise from the ground line to the top of the wall, but this is not commonplace except in stone walls. Further, when the site's slope forces you to follow a noticeably ascending or descending grade, such as that presented by a pitched walk or driveway, you should install 90-degree steps between sections for architecturally crisp and correct visual appeal.

With a fieldstone retaining wall, whether laid dry or with neatly mortared joints sealing one stone to another (preferably deep-set joints to emphasize the

Horse fencing backed with thin mesh equally manages outward views and safety enclosure.

Crisp step-ups enhance the attractiveness of this well-made wall.

interlocked stones), any moisture caused by the weather or from the soil behind the wall must be allowed to quickly drain away to forestall buckling of the structure. In any unmortared or dry wall construction the many open joints between stones easily resolve this drainage problem, although some masons include as an extra precaution a narrow layer of small stones along the entirety of the rear of the wall down to the base. A mortar-sealed stone wall, on the other hand, requires not only this loose-stone drainage treatment but also the inclusion of mesh-covered, 2-inch diameter metal or plastic pipes—called weep holes—stretching through the wall about 6 inches above the final grade elevation at even intervals of between 8 and 10 feet along its length. These practical drain pipes should not protrude beyond the wall frontage. A free-standing stone wall, which should be mortared for reliable stability, does not require weep holes or any other special drainage treatment, of course.

Another design consideration for either a retaining or free-standing stone wall is the angle of repose of every stone used. This means that you or your mason has to review and consistently interpret how each stone can be best placed for its shape, color, and size to blend artistically with its neighbors. Building a superior-looking stone wall is, indeed, a thoughtful process—as well as a tedious one. A free-standing stone wall is even more demanding of time and effort because it must be finished handsomely on two visible sides as well as on each boundary corner. Such walls are likely to become quite wide to allow for these many visible stones to be fitted together without the added expense of having to chip or saw them. This may explain why many free-standing walls are composed of uniform brick rather than stone.

Because an individual brick is small and lightweight compared to stone, the interlocking units cannot be taken to great heights—or used independently as a retaining wall—without a support core of cement concrete created ahead of time. Obviously, in such cases the brick is actually just a veneer finish to what is in fact a substantial concrete wall. Even so, its construction still requires the inclusion of weep holes, as described above for mortared stone walls. A low, free-standing brick wall of 3 or 4 feet, however, would not need any cement core for strength but can likely be made three-bricks wide, and even perforated in a variety of interesting patterns.

The continued durability and proper plumbness of any type of wall is highly dependent upon the construction of the in-ground footing or base on which it stands—or wobbles. Normally built slightly wider than the intended wall dimension, and most often made from poured cement concrete on a firm bed of loose stones or gravel, this subsurface footing may have to be installed at a bottom level up to 3 feet deep in very cold climates. For frost-free areas the footing depth location would be reduced dramatically. Another point to remember is that a wall cannot successfully endure if constructed on sizable sections of newly filled earth since both the earth and the wall will soon settle and crack. Proper soil firmness is always essential.

Walls of stone or brick endure longer when they are kept as weather-dry as possible, especially protected from wind-driven rain that may eventually seep inside and then freeze in place. Waterproof mortar is helpful, of course, but a durable capping across the top of the wall is even more valuable. Slightly tilted, flat stone pieces or cemented brick courses can act as protective umbrellas here for redirecting the rain, particularly if this finish treatment is allowed to overhang the face of the wall itself. A dry-laid, boulder wall does not need this rain protection for any practical need, but a topping of thin, cut stone can add an attractive, decorative touch.

Distinctively pierced brickwork provides a practical and attractive enclosure for this urban garden.

Wood is another popular building material for either free-standing or retaining walls, including large planter boxes acting as grade supports. Considered welcoming for the built-in compatibility with nearby plants, wood construction items that are sophisticated-looking are generally assembled from trimmed hardwoods such as redwood in thick, wide boards tightly set together horizontally. These butted planks are attached to a sturdy background frame of similar wood firmly anchored into the ground. Especially attractive for contemporary garden settings, the completed wall can be simply sealed with a wood preservative or else left to weather naturally—although to a different color value. Such constructions can also be painted, but since retaining walls often have so much moisture behind the wood, the paint is likely to flake off in a short time.

Primarily utilized for rustic-looking retaining walls—but rarely for free-standing ones—old railroad ties are also suitable construction materials where readily available cheaply. (Unused ties have no rail spike holes and are marketed as "industrial ties" in some areas.) Heavy in weight (up to 175 pounds) and sizable in length (up to 9 feet), these ties are modest-sized hardwood trees planed into 9-inch-wide, mostly rectangular outlines. They are fully protected against

Redwood walls and planter boxes create a contemporary emphasis for a Boston courtyard.

decay right to their centers by prior boiling in oily, gunky creosote for hours. Railroad ties can be found in many lumber yards and garden centers as deep brown logs, which cannot be stained or painted, of variable shape and condition. Reducing the size of the ties for particular site needs is best managed with a power or chain saw, but be alert that the ends often have sturdy metal cleats, which were originally included to forestall splitting of the ties. As with any other retaining wall, railroad ties require an underground, stable footing down to the known frost line. This can be accomplished by laying additional ties horizontally on a uniform bed of gravel or crushed stone, both for improved drainage as well as for ease in setting the ties levelly. A cement concrete base has no purpose with railroad ties. To anchor one layer to another, drive in foot-long, spiral-grooved spikes at an angle using a power hammer, which is much less wearying than hand-driving. Since these ties have somewhat irregular surfaces, which fit snugly but not totally flat against each other, weep holes are not needed, but it is still advantageous to add a narrow backfill of loose stones behind the entire wall down to ground level.

If the proposed wall is intended to be higher than 4 feet and longer than 10

A railroad-tie wall comfortably fits this woodland setting on Cape Cod, Massachusetts.

feet, then you need to include additional 5- or 6-foot ties perpendicular to the face of the wall in each of the layers for every 6 to 8 feet of length. This special design treatment helps anchor the soil and maintains the stability and plumbness of the wall by counteracting the constant pressure of water-laden soil to bulge or tilt the wall forward. Nevertheless, before you begin such a project be certain that this anchoring technique will not be seriously encumbered by major tree roots or large rock outcrops. If it is so handicapped, you may be better off installing a simpler-to-erect, but costlier, masonry support wall.

Fences

Years ago, Robert Frost wrote: "Good fences make good neighbors." His astute observation must have pleased a large audience because thousands of differently useful fences now are evident everywhere. A fence does have a practical function on just about all homeowner lots since it can serve either as a barrier to unwanted entry (or against escape of small children and pets), a noticeable boundary marker, a wind deflector, a screen to eliminate unwelcome views, or just a decorative garden addition. All these assets can apply equally to a wall or a dense hedge, of course, but fencing has a special characteristic that neither of the other design elements can easily match: narrowness.

Whether constructed of wood, bamboo, framed plastic, or metal, a fence typically takes up less width space than any wall or hedge, and it can fit into many constricted and difficult areas that the others could not. Fencing is also especially appealing because it normally costs far less than an equally long and high wall and can usually be erected within a briefer time and with less effort. Nevertheless, wood and bamboo are not permanent materials (metal is very durable) and require additional maintenance by the not-uncommon need for replacement parts on a regular basis. Depending upon its particular location and function, a fence of wood or metal may require frequent painting or staining to maintain a fresh appearance and enhance its setting. In more rustic areas a wood fence can be left to weather naturally, but some metal fencing will still need regular painting to prevent corrosion.

Except from a public safety standpoint, fences or walls are not usually regulated by legal ordinances for their basic construction materials, but acceptable heights are commonly established by local laws, which vary from community to community. Such rules apply most often to constructions either on or very close to property lines as well as to solid, street-corner barriers, which might possibly obscure traffic dangers. Check well beforehand with the local building authority to avoid future problems about legal conformance. Of course, you can always apply for a variance to build differently from adopted ordinances, but this is sometimes a slow process and offers no guarantee of success.

Just like walls, fences are also architectural additions to a garden scene and should artistically maintain a scale and style that is compatible with their surroundings. Any fence, particularly if a complex design statement, will have the greatest visual appeal when established on as level a platform as possible, and any needed grading adjustments should be done well ahead of time. Where noticeable grade changes are impossible to correct without great cost, however, a useful design technique is to incorporate regular, 90-degree steps into the fence layout to maintain visual strength—just as you would do with a masonry wall.

This trim kitchen garden fence needs only minimal painting attention for durability.

Whether your design choice is open pickets, a solid stockade, or even metal uprights, a fence has strongly vertical elements that require consistent architectural plumbness. Following existing, irregular grading will produce a weak and unsatisfactory visual impact, and the top of the fence will definitely show an unlevel, rolling profile that surely was not intended. When in doubt about the ground's levelness, stretch a simple line level to a taut twine strung between stakes and then make any needed adjustments either to the soil or to the proposed fence layout. One modification is to raise the entire fence—or several sections depending upon the complications of grading—and add earth fill beneath. Another resolution is to trim off a few inches from the less-noticed bottom end of the pickets or palings on the higher ground, or else do the reverse by using longer pickets or palings on the down-sloping earth, in both cases maintaining a level top. The horse fence is an approach that works satisfactorily on both flat and very rolling terrain. Its ribbonlike layout provides a comfortable visual effect as it logically parallels the topography, over hill, dale, or flatness. Such a fence is simple to erect, economical, and totally effective as a gentle barrier on many sites (see pages 75, 81, and 171).

Regular steps in this wood fencing create visual harmony on a sloping site.

The most commonly used material for fencing is wood, both for its lower cost compared to masonry as well as for its availability to carpenter or handy-man. Kiln-dried lumber is the best choice to minimize warping, and all assembling should be with rust- and corrosion-proof nails or screws. Greater durability—though also greater cost—comes with knot-free board and post selections of one of various wood types, and the in-ground ends of the support posts benefit from prior rot-prevention treatment. A special asset of wood is the ease with which it can be cut to fit, either by the supplier or on the job, to create any number of complex arrangements in historic styles or contemporary interpretations.

Keep in mind that any aboveground wood parts such as cross rails or upright palings in direct contact with moist earth or plant mulch will quickly turn spongy and eventually decay even if originally painted or stained. This problem is due to the ever-present activity of soil bacteria that continually feed on the cellulose in wood, so you should avoid creating a food pantry here by simply raising the bottom line of the fence several inches above the final surface treatment, whether open soil or mulch. In brief, always leave reasonable air spaces around

Intricate historic designs are readily managed with wood fencing details.

exposed wood. Yes, some people worry that invading animal life can then sneak through these bottom openings, but if that is a prominent concern, nail some galvanized wire mesh as a consistent barrier along the entire fence bottom. This mesh will soon disappear from noticeable view with normal weathering or the growth of nearby plants.

Dried bamboo cane is a popular and economical fencing material often seen decorating tropical and semi-tropical garden settings. These stems especially enhance the mood of an Oriental design layout with their neutral color value and delicate texture. A member of the grass family, bamboo is sold in a variety of diameters and can be assembled for attractive fencing in a number of ways. When split or hammered, the parts can be woven into solid mats attached to a sturdy set of horizontal, full-cane rails, which are then anchored to heavier bamboo posts. The upright posts should be capped to keep the rain out of the almost-hollow interior. Premade fencing can also be purchased in stylistic variations of open latticework, all tied together with durable twine or thin wire. Since all bamboo constructions are relatively lightweight compared to wood, they are not meant for locations where wind gusts are strong and consistent. Unfortunately, these tropical plant parts are also not especially durable in the coldest regions since they quickly split or disintegrate in consistent frost. Where logically adapted for garden use, however, bamboo fencing contributes a remarkably subtle and desirable garden accent of special worth.

Large sheets of translucent, preferably colorless plastic, when mounted in durable wood frames, can give a fascinating new meaning to the term "solid" in privacy fencing. Such non-clear panels obscure direct viewing in or out, but they also provide an additional bonus of subdued lighting to a setting, along with possible dancing shadows created by planting behind the screen. When subtly backlit these panels can supply a soft glow to enhance evening viewing. Easy to keep clean, the smooth or pebbled surfaces of such relatively thin, lightweight pieces normally have remarkable resistance to dangerous shattering and to disintegration from intense sunlight. Their use in gardens can promote either a contemporary or an Oriental look.

Similar in handling but different in function, tempered and mesh-encased clear glass panels can be placed as wind barriers around some areas of exposed swimming pools or terraces. These clear sections extend the view but do not provide privacy. They are held in place most often by slender, corrosion-resistant metal support frames down to the ground or pavement level or else can be mounted atop a brick wall foundation of any necessary height.

Metal fencing can be a substantial, yet nearly invisible, deterrent to easy access for both city and country properties, whether in the utilitarian chain-link style or in highly decorative units displaying historic or contemporary detailing. With metal's built-in strength even in thin-wrought pieces, such fencing material provides the twin bonuses of greater ventilation and open viewing opportunities without compromising safety or site suitability. The openwork metal fences (solid metal sheets are rarely used) are normally less obvious than wood fencing might be. This is due, of course, to the usual slenderness of the various parts as well as to the subdued, almost-vanishing appearance of metal fences painted in the typically dark colors tradition seems to require for garden correctness. These deep colorings sensibly and effectively diminish fence outlines into a shadowy presence, but if you prefer to highlight your fencing to create a

Plastic-panel fencing creates dancing shadows while reinterpreting the concept of "solid" in privacy enclosure.

specific effect, then you should substitute brighter color values in careful harmony with the setting.

Constructed mainly from forged wrought iron, mild steel or bronze bars, cast iron, or even aluminum, metal fences take up relatively little ground space but do carry a more expensive price tag than fences of other materials. All metal forms have a stability and durability well beyond that of wood or bamboo constructions, and the maintenance needs are minimal, consisting mostly of re-painting to combat rust on iron or steel. Aluminum fencing does not rust but can become pitted over the years. Rust-free bronze is undoubtedly the easiest to handle since it can be left to weather slowly to a richer, deeper tone while maintaining excellent smoothness to the touch. Bronze fencing, however, is the most expensive metal used in fencing.

Metal also allows for a wide variety of complex and personalized design interpretations matched by no other fencing material. It can be shaped, molded, hammered, or even layered into a rich set of choices, but quality artisans to do this special work are neither plentiful nor inexpensive. Even though many pre-fabricated metal items are certainly serviceable and economically attractive, any importantly featured metalwork should look both substantial and worth its

Some Victorian cast-iron fencing offers three-dimensional interest.

cost. If you are hampered by a tight budget—or even if you are not—consider searching out interesting older pieces from local architectural salvage yards, keeping a keen eye to recognize how a little rehabilitation can bring a true bargain.

Antique cast-iron fencing sections, especially those popular during Victorian times that show reliefs of vines, flowers, or tree trunks, can introduce shadowline appeal and whimsical interest to many garden layouts, whether your design concept is a period restoration or an avant-garde experiment. As with all garden details, fencing can be a memorable and personally inventive expression of design value that goes far beyond its basic need.

Walks and Steps

Every walk should logically provide a safe, comfortable, and pleasant passageway, but the one leading to the front door of a house should not only direct your footsteps easily but also bring attention to the accompanying, welcoming garden design scheme. From a practical standpoint this main walk should undoubtedly be paved with stone, brick, or cement concrete. Because this entryway is used in all kinds of weather, it should be solid underfoot, nonslippery, generous in width, properly illuminated, and fitted harmoniously into its surroundings. The walk should also provide a convenient and logical sense of direction without any odd meanderings. Naturally, these basic objectives apply in some manner to all other walks and paths throughout your grounds.

The architectural style of a house should importantly influence the outline, surface texture, and color harmony of an approach walk. A formalized setting promotes a crisp design layout of tailored paving pieces at right-angled joint connections and often neatly curbed, while an informal presentation suggests a more relaxed, curvilinear approach with, perhaps, mildly irregular edges and a somewhat roughened surface. The size and character of the house should also determine the proper width for this walk. A stately home demands a proportionately grand sweep of handsome paving, not a skimpy path, yet a less imposing dwelling can be well served by a minimal width of about 3 feet. At no point, however, should you seriously consider having an entry walk made only of random-sized stepstones margined by tufts of grass lawn. This all-too-common design error will quickly become dangerous as trapped rainwater (or ice), along with too many visitors' feet, will cause the stones to slowly sink and the turf to clump up around them. Stepstone paths should be reserved for passageways with only occasional use.

Careful initial preparation of a porous base to act as an in-ground drainage system is vital to the continued stability of any walk. This detail involves providing an even layer at least 6 inches deep (more if hard frosts or excessive moisture are characteristics of your site) of compacted coarse sand, gravel, stone dust, or any other hard and permanent material capable of heavy compression without totally solidifying. If the walk surface is laid dry (without mortar), then you will benefit by including dual curbing edges to restrain these loose pieces from eventually sliding sideways. With mortared joints you can omit any curbing, other than for decorative purposes, but you will require a cement concrete base (possibly reinforced by steel rods) atop the sub-base of sand or gravel, which in turn will need to be placed deeper to accommodate the new concrete pad. All mortared walkways are the province of a reliable contractor and are not considered readily workable for homeowner installation.

This focused entry walk and steps are complemented by proper lighting and harmonious plantings.

Choices for rigid, weatherproof walk materials are highly varied, depending upon your local climate as well as your budget, and common options include utilitarian asphalt, plain cement concrete, quarried stone of various colors, hard-fired brick (not soft chimney brick), weatherproof tile, water-rounded pebbles in a mastic base, hardwood lumber, or wood blocks. Each has a different aesthetic, cost factor, life span, and site appropriateness. When combining different types into an individualistic design, you should limit yourself to no more than two harmonious selections to avoid visual confusion or fussiness. Remember, too, that a welcoming pattern for a walk does not automatically arrive by your choice of materials but only by an artistic arrangement of them.

Whether elegant or rustic in design, steps can be major additions to a garden scene, depending upon the setting and the frequency of use. As a convenient and utilitarian means of moving yourself comfortably from one elevation to another (and often additionally as extra seating), steps can be created from many different building materials. Each set should logically harmonize, of course, in scale, color value, and texture with any connecting walk or adjacent terrace. In addition, steps require unslick tops that shed rainfall or melting snow easily, especially in well-traveled areas.

Rounded pebbles set in durable mastic show imaginative styling here.

These steps are well-integrated with the adjacent terraces. Deliberately overscaled, they can also provide occasional casual seating.

Weathered wood steps and walk handsomely merge in this yellow-foliaged entryway.

Because outdoor steps are constantly exposed to a variety of climatic changes, they should not follow the steep riser heights customarily used indoors. Your maximum riser outdoors should be limited to 6 inches high and the accompanying tread should be no less than 12 inches wide, with shorter risers and wider treads for a more leisurely gait where the preferred site and available space allow. To establish quicker recognition of the quantity of steps, as well as to add attractive shadow lines, include an overhanging lip of at least one inch for each tread, whether the steps are made from stone, brick, or wood. Poured cement concrete steps, left plain, normally do not carry such overhanging lips, nor do sizable, quarried stone pieces.

Avoid incorporating a single step anywhere since it is rarely noticed, much to the dismay of a toppling guest. Plan always to have multiple steps for greater safety. For ease of use, a long flight of eight or more steps should be broken up at its midpoint with a proportionately sized landing, and consider adding side handrails. Also be sure to integrate adequate night lighting near any entry site that includes steps. Your guests will appreciate such thoughtfulness.

Terraces and Decks

A well-conceived terrace can add the year-round pleasure of outdoor entertaining and dining to every houselot. Whether small or large, this well-enjoyed garden feature always invites relaxed use by every age group. Although "terrace" and "patio" are currently accepted as interchangeable terms, that is not quite the case technically. A terrace is a relatively flat, raised platform normally found close to a building—a house, pool cabana, or pavilion, for example—and is potentially open on three sides and surfaced with turf, paving, or some combination. A patio, on the other hand, is a walled, paved, inner courtyard open only to the sky and found closely associated with the main dwelling. Terraces, then, are more often affiliated with the landscape openness of suburban and country settings, while patios are more likely to be city-oriented features.

Rather than simply replacing skimpy grass with durable paving to be rid of a nagging mud problem, you should focus your design concerns in broader directions. First, plan a size sufficient not only for the number of regular users but for several guests as well, along with adequate space for the appropriate furniture. Then look for a site that maximizes privacy, provides reliable cross ventilation, has protection (either existing or easily introduced) from excessive sun or strong wind, produces quick surface drainage, maintains convenient access to and from the house, and last but hardly least, offers attractive views of your own garden spaces. Of course, you should not feel restricted to only one terraced layout if there are sufficient reasons and available land for more than one. Good ideas are worth repeating.

The simplest formula for creating an outdoor sitting and eating area is to position furniture on a parcel of flattish ground that has a thick turf cover able to withstand some abuse. Nevertheless, furniture placed in a fixed location on the lawn will shade the grass beneath it, causing some noticeable thinness and off-coloring unless you frequently shift the pieces around. Foot scuffing of the turf fronting the chairs is also a constant concern. All-grass terraces, then, are often better managed with only occasional furniture use, and the more lightweight such pieces are, the easier your set up for social get-togethers will be. Including some pavement is the wiser option.

Durable paved surfaces of brick, stone, cement concrete, or weatherproof tile readily avoid the maintenance concerns associated with grass turf, and they

This sunny, brick-covered terrace is perched high above a woodlot glen.

are the most frequently used construction materials today. With any of these surfaces, your furniture needs to be set up only once, or it can be moved about and left wherever necessary—a true convenience. Paving naturally absorbs and holds more heat from the sun than grass, which means providing some occasional shading by nearby trees is an important comfort consideration. Paved terraces with plantings within them need generously sized soil areas to catch rainfall if the paving joints are mortared, and you may even have to provide additional irrigation as the plants expand their roots into the pavement base. Dry-laid constructions, however, have open joints that allow for greater moisture to reach any plant roots below, but here, too, you may have to supply additional seasonal water as the plants grow and roots expand.

Whether a terrace shape should be angular or curved is partly determined by the architectural style of the adjacent house or outbuilding, as well as, of course, by your own design intentions. Either outline can prove satisfactory, but you should first stake out the proposed layout to evaluate its visual and practical appeal in actual dimensions. More important than the shape, however, is the ultimate size of the terrace. As a simple guideline for floor footage, allow 36 square

Introduced trees here provide shade that encourages frequent outdoor dining.

feet for each person regularly utilizing the area. Each 6-by-6-foot unit here provides space for people, a normal mix of outdoor furniture, and a modest passageway for moving about. (Parties, to be sure, produce amiable crowding no matter how large your terrace.) For a family of six, this basic terrace area approximates a rectangle 20 feet long by 10 feet wide. Naturally, the bulkiness or daintiness of your furniture affects usable outdoor space, so choose carefully to avoid an overscaled look, the same way you would select furniture for indoors.

In determining the appropriate furniture, pay close attention to how much vivid or patterned cushion material you use so as to avoid disturbing the serenity of the setting. What we find attractive under showroom lights may not be quite as commendable when it reaches the great outdoors. Quietly tasteful decor will always be more favorable here, particularly since it may be surrounded by a wealth of colors and designs offered by seasonal flowers and other plantings. Just keep in mind that outdoor furniture is largely static and un-

This concrete terrace serves six users well.

When it comes to selecting a deck color, you have the option of leaving the boards and safety rails to weather naturally to silvery gray, or else you can stain them in a tone compatible with the surroundings. Avoid painting any deck since the paint usually flakes and chips all too readily. As a final note, keep all free-standing planter pots or boxes elevated several inches above the deck to avoid wood rot or water stains. As with wood fencing, maintain open air around all deck parts to forestall such potential problems as warping, rotting, or decay.

Outdoor Rooms

Spatial divisions within a house are called rooms and are normally enclosed by divider walls, bringing privacy to certain activities. Each individual space there potentially allows for both the expected and unexpected interior treatment in dimensions and decor for personal use. If you transfer this same evaluation to a garden development, any enclosed or partially obscured area with a special purpose can be labeled an outdoor room. A fenced or hedged vegetable garden is a simplified but commonly seen (or not seen) example of a utilitarian outdoor

This outdoor room offers quiet and private dining away from the main garden areas.

room. Isolating a garden space when it produces off-season emptiness is a practical reason for such year-round screening. A well-shielded overlook with accommodations for outdoor dining is another instance of special hideaway appeal offering a pleasant surprise to the unknowing visitor.

Of course, you already have space definitions for your property when you simply refer to the front, rear, and side yards, but these spaces are not considered outdoor rooms, even if one area is called the children's playfield and another the cookout post. Missing here are the special dimensions of mystery, surprise, and personal creativity—the same stimulating ingredients you employ when furnishing a house. Outdoor rooms of any size are more fulfilling when they become surprising spaces with unique embellishments and uses.

A prominent consideration in planning an outdoor room should be the production of a mood response that encourages a relaxed withdrawal from nearby distractions. In an effectively designed outdoor room, you should experience a sense of visual and physical comfort, with a genuine impulse to pause for a while

Impeccable Oriental-style detailing offers calm diversion in this secluded outdoor room.

to absorb the details of the setting. Discovering some seating placed conveniently at hand always adds to the pleasure.

What you select as the focus in your half-hidden oasis is strictly up to you and can involve a wealth of design opportunities from unusual planting selections, dramatic construction elements, or a collection of unique artifacts. A subtly arranged and finely executed walkway through an Oriental-inspired garden, for example, can offer a well-appreciated, relaxing diversion, further embellished with a decorative gateway set into a surrounding screening hedge. It offers a quiet yet compelling mood.

At my present home I arranged an outdoor room at the rear of the lot by discarding a bramble mess that I had tolerated for years since I had had no other special need for the space. But I eventually realized I could benefit from another shaded sitting area, and this one offered a long view of the main lawn and its col-

A private "Hidden Garden" retreat on the author's prop...

orful shrub beds, a view not available elsewhere on the property. Once cleared, the area was only 30 feet long and 20 feet deep, but it was nicely backed by a dense thicket of volunteer seedling trees and native shrubs on my neighbor's land, which gave sufficient privacy. After improving the soil for planned shrub and perennial introductions, I laid out a wide, semicircular pathway for two-way access to the adjacent lawn and coated it with a heavy layer of soft, pine-bark mulch. Next I planted a shade-producing crabapple tree and a backdrop screen of various shade-tolerant, flowering evergreen and deciduous shrubs with staggered blooming times, all interwoven with collections of perennials and bulbs not found elsewhere in my garden.

To encourage more than just a walk-through of this planted gem, I introduced some black, ironwork chairs and a low table along with a small, trickling fountain. This total combination, once discovered, invites stopping, lingering, and lounging. Each season offers some special planting interest in color and fragrance.

Because of the additional placement of some carefully arranged, medium-sized shrubs at the foreground of the space, the contents of this retreat are invisible from the living room windows directly across the intervening lawn. But to ensure that a guest independently strolling the grounds is gently reminded to make a visit, I added a modest-sized, smooth fieldstone marker with the legend "Hidden Garden" carved into it at the usual approach end of the interior path. Although you do have to find and experience the quiet revelations of this remote space for yourself, it lives up to the basic premise of a designed setting illustrating specialized separateness.

Proportionate Size in Plants and Construction

Any woody plant enlarges in size annually, and even if it seems unlikely when you make a skinny addition to your garden, every young plant will soon become greater in height and width, changing the landscape scene. Knowing beforehand what to expect from growth will readily guide you toward the cor-

The rear lot of the author's property, facing east, at initial planting.

The same scene three years later.

rect spacing and help prevent overgrown intrusion later. Plants should always complement the site and buildings, which requires that the eventual size of all plant material be appropriately in proportion since the site structures are unlikely to enlarge dramatically, if at all.

While a multistory house with appropriate land area can easily accommodate large plant masses to match its volume, a one-story building normally appears more comfortable with smaller-sized mature plantings. Keep in mind that you can prune back unwanted growth only so much before the plants becomes artificial-looking and formalized. If the plants do not have built-in proportions of slower growth, pruning chores can be unending and costly. Wise initial selection and placement provides for less upkeep later.

Garden structures such as walls, steps, fences, walks, terraces, and decks need to follow a similar set of guidelines for appropriate proportions, as do ornamental accents contributed by a fountain, statue, bench, or even outdoor furniture (see Chapter 5 for details). Every element of the created garden influences all others, without exception. Having just one item oversized or undersized for its location can immediately—and perhaps lastingly—disturb the intended harmony of the whole. If you have any doubts about the end result of a combination, and whether it will be truly proportionate, rethink your initial idea. Professionals do this just as frequently as amateurs, since few find the complete answer to a complex problem on the first try.

Form in Plants and Construction

The form or natural mass of a plant, whether large- or modest-sized at maturity, contributes a continual visual impact to a garden design. Evergreens, of course, bring year-round solidness with their silhouettes, while deciduous plants only have bulk during the growing season. The built forms provided by a fence, wall, fountain, arbor, or teahouse are also year-round elements of a design and can capture the eye by their shape and placement. Planting and construction, then, must be combined carefully so as to complement each other at all times, whether by similarity or contrast of forms. (See also Chapter 9.)

An important difference between these two major design elements, however, is that the planting will expand over time while the construction will remain static. That is why it is critical to understand beforehand the plants' rate of growth if you wish to maintain a proper balance. It is always a great disappointment to have structures or other nearby plants overwhelmed by unneeded, vigorous growth even if the basic forms were correctly chosen and harmoniously positioned. Take the time to learn how a decade of normal growth will affect your carefully proportioned, intended garden layout. Proper initial plant selection, not severe pruning later, is the proper approach here.

Texture in Plants and Construction

For most construction items, texture refers to the appearance and arrangement of surfaces, but for plants it also extends to include leaf and flower size in defining the coarseness or fineness in each of the seasons. Small-leaved trees such as the evergreen hemlock (*Tsuga*) and deciduous honeylocust (*Gleditsia*) carry fine-textured foliage, while the large leaves of the defoliating catalpa and deciduous magnolia have coarse textures, and even their blossoming is sizable. Among evergreen shrubs, all the yew (*Taxus*) types have delicately slender, short needles, yet the majority of rhododendrons commonly present broad, elon-

This garden scene effectively combines contrasting forms in construction and plantings.

gated leaf clusterings. Garden perennials such as peony and hosta have conspicuously bold foliage, in contrast with the daintiness of heather (*Calluna*) and maidenhair fern (*Adiantum*). Every geographic region has a similar variety of plants for textural interest. Even when out of flower, plants offer considerable visual stimulation to a garden scene.

With regard to construction items, you should investigate ahead of time the texture that you wish to have imparted by the structure and its construction technique. A brick wall, for example, conveys a smooth, fine textural appearance due to its evenly laid, equal-sized pieces, but the natural roughness and irregular jointing of a farmer-styled, fieldstone wall provides a coarser texture. As an-

Textural differences between the yew (*Taxus*) hedge and rhododendron shrub in the foreground provide visual contrast.

other example, the decorative cast-iron fencing of Victorian times, with irregular plant and flower shapes, presents a roughened texture as well as some chunkiness in general outline. A distinctly different effect is offered by the very slender, almost invisible, and slick smoothness of looped metal railings. Split-rail wood fences, with their wavy profiles and unplaned surfaces, convey a coarser look than the uniform delicacy of bamboo screening. Whatever your textural choice, make certain it is in visual harmony with its location.

A mix of plant textures is far easier to resolve because so many choices are currently available in every growing area, whereas with construction materials the options are more limited. The construction technique, therefore, often is crucial for the most attractive expression of your design intentions. For example, mortared stone walls look best with neatly uniform cement joints, not slathered by excess mortar obscuring the individual stones. Paved terraces, too, visually benefit from commonly repeated jointing as well as identical colorings from the chosen paving material. Look for local examples of desirable walls, fences, gates, arbors, terraces, and the like, and then carefully go over your own interpretation with the builder. Every artisan creates a personalized system of construction techniques, so make sure that you both are clear from the beginning what the end result is to be.

Placement of Plants and Construction

The placement of plants, construction, or decorative artifacts often determines how far the eye will travel across a space before it stops. That is why we enjoy the seashore, with its seemingly unlimited horizon that allows us to literally see for miles. Every garden design benefits from a sense of outdoor spaciousness, too, along with a sense of visual flow, inviting investigation of what lies around each corner. Oversized, bushy plants placed too close to a house will create a closed-in feeling for the interior as well as the exterior and likely will eliminate any views but the backsides of entangled stems. This overall sense of spaciousness and flow is another important reason why you should be aware of the proportions and future growth habits of plants in determining their initial placement, and not crowd them for an immediate effect.

Be careful as well about the placement of a tree, an outbuilding, or a statue in an open area, since these objects will interrupt and foreshorten the spaces

The rear lot of the author's property, facing west, at start of planting in early spring.

The same scene three years later, in summer.

around them as well as halt your view beyond. While a handsome item located close at hand allows for greater appreciation of it, improper placement can significantly reduce the outdoor space, and you will not gain the highest return on your design investment. Remember, too, that any introduced object likely will require additional plantings in its vicinity for visual support, and this will take up even more space. As always, plan for the total site compatability of a project before you focus on the details.

Color Harmony in Plants and Construction

Plant coloration changes seasonally with new growth, flower bloom, fruit or cone crops, and autumn foliage displays, but the basic color of any construction generally remains static except for weathering effects or repainting. Garden artifacts such as a fountain, statue, or set of urns gain the patina of age but otherwise stay unchanged. Since plantings are the major variable in a garden setting, you do well to observe their contributions to adjacent objects, especially on a year-round basis, and if any plant choice is not truly harmonious, it is best simply to relocate it (see also Chapter 6).

A red brick house, for example, will always present a particular tone of red, but if its emphasis were challenged by a springtime mass of noncomplementary flaming red azaleas, then the plants should be reassigned to another location. The color of the fixed building should always dominate, as should that of any other constructed item or important artifact. Drive around your neighborhood in different seasons to check out how your proposed color combinations look on other properties to learn which are agreeable with your own ideas. I call this the "free-peek" approach to garden design, and it can be very rewarding.

Chapter 4

*

Creating a Site Program

As the years pass, some changes, whether minor or major, to your home grounds are inevitable. This might mean simply adding trees for additional shade or planting shrubs to block out a disliked view. It also might entail expanding existing beds to gain extra color, fragrance, or textural interest. Your plantings may now be overgrown, take too much time and effort to maintain, or just be in the way of some needed space for a new terrace, additional parking, or perhaps a swimming pool. Any of these situations are a normal part of our lives as we constantly seek improvements to our surroundings, yet the best and most complete answer to some site problems may require more detailed evaluation well before you begin. Creating a map of your existing conditions can greatly assist your efforts.

Making a Map

Even if you are one of those lucky enough to have the ability to visualize clearly what your current landscape will soon become, you can still benefit from making a plan on paper beforehand. For one, you will more easily comprehend the existing interrelationships of the spaces, and you can clearly indicate on such a map which items are to be preserved, relocated, modified, or even eliminated. This annotated map can also become a useful site-clearing drawing for a contractor, while also providing you with the basic facts to study at your leisure the proposed garden development. While map-making may sound like a bit of work—and it is—it is far less expensive and time-consuming than having to debate what to do next while a contractor's crew and bulldozer are already meandering around the site. A good map, accompanied by a good design scheme, pays off quickly.

The official location or deed map of a property is often called a plot plan—it is usually provided at the closing of the sale on a house or property. Because plot plans are normally printed at a very small scale, you may find it most useful to have it enlarged at a photo shop or blueprint office so that you can make clear, readable jottings. For further convenience, make several copies, since they are very inexpensive.

This basic plot plan will normally show a north point, property lines, the house position (along with any other taxable structures), plus street and driveway locations, together with a measurement scale. Make sure that the scale is accurate, since maps are now often reduced to fit into municipal binders, thus making the printed scale unusable. Test this out by actually measuring if a scaled inch equals an actual inch. If it does not, then you should seek out a copy of the original map.

What a typical plot plan will *not* reveal is the location of any existing plantings, underground utility connections or buried oil tanks, land contours, or the positioning of walls, fences, and walks. That useful data either you have to provide by measuring and noting the features yourself, or else pay a surveyor to create a new topographic map of all the site features you want included (in which case you can obviously omit making your own site survey map). While a topographic map is not inexpensive, it will provide usefully detailed information more easily and with greater accuracy, especially if the existing land has complex grading or contains many plant masses.

If you choose to collect this site information on your own, which is usually not overly complicated, first find two 50- or 100-foot tapes and a helper to hold one end of each tape as you maneuver about (to save some time). When forced to measure solo, however, bring along two sturdy screwdrivers to anchor the tapes in the ground by poking them through the open tabs at the ends. Leave the enlarged plot plan indoors and, instead, take graph paper on a clipboard for these field measurements. Transfer the notes later to the plot plan, using identical scales for both. Next, roughly pace the extent of the survey area to verify it will fit on the graph paper. If not, attach additional sheets.

Start your measuring from a convenient house corner already drawn on the paper. Add the rest of the measured house outline as needed. To check that the tape is properly parallel with the house wall, position your head against this wall a few feet back from the corner and sight along the tape. Your eyes will tell you of any needed adjustment. It's simple but it works. Now locate and record the distance to your first item. Aim for some major object such as a tree, wall, fence, or outbuilding in direct line with the extended tape, which now becomes the "base line." Items located perpendicular from this base line become "offsets," which are measured lines drawn at right angles from the base. This explains the need for two tapes here. If the angle produced to reach the offset is smaller or larger than the required 90 degrees, reposition the second tape along the base line until it conforms. Now measure and record both the base line distance from the corner and the offset distance. Continue using this technique until you have completed the area survey.

By now you might have surmised that each offset alignment relates closely to why the right-angled lines of the graph paper are useful. In a sense you are creating an invisible grid on the land, which allows you to make any number of measurements offset from the established base line. Transferring the starting point from one house corner to another does not alter your approach. Your finished product may not be as precise as a surveyor's plan, but it will readily serve your needs for generalized garden design studies. Just be certain that you faithfully record all the measurements accurately, or else you may have to redo the work later. With mapping by professional or amateur, accuracy is the only criterion.

Once you have transferred your field notes to the plot plan, you then need to make other site reviews with it. On a sunny day take the plan outdoors at different times (which should be recorded) and mark which areas are consistently bright, which tend to be semishaded, and which are stuck in the gloom of a nearby building or tall, evergreen trees. On a rainy day (sorry) verify where the surface water travels across and out of your property, and then add directional arrows on the plan. If water stagnates and puddles anywhere, note the size of that area as well. Under these moist conditions, protect your drawing either with a plastic shield or have a helper tote a sheltering umbrella.

If possible, locate and roughly measure any septic leaching field or buried oil tank, since you will not be able to install any large-scale planting above such spots. Locating underground gas, water, and sewer lines will require the assistance of the utility companies, but including these on your map can help prevent planting conflicts later. Shade trees and overhead utility wires do not make comfortable companions either, especially if the utility company has the right to remove major branches. A hollow-pruned tree is not a visual joy in any landscape, so be alert to where you position new trees. As you can probably tell by now, the more comprehensive your amended plot plan is, the greater the benefit when you lay out the intended development ideas.

Exploring a Basic Layout

With all the basic site information carefully plotted to scale on the plot plan you can now spend time studying what design changes you want. On tracing paper, freely sketch in pencil (easier to erase than ink), and retain all your various studies until the end, since you just might return to an earlier proposal. Do not rush to any conclusions until you have tested more than one set of initial ideas. Then spend time reviewing and modifying your concepts until all the parts work together harmoniously, trying out new proportions to address any problems. All professionals design and evaluate their projects by this trial-and-error approach, too.

Next test out your rough studies on the ground where the changes will eventually be made. Use highly visible wood stakes to indicate the outlines of proposed planting beds, sites for specimen trees or hedges, water features, intended walls, fences, and walks, or whatever else you wish to include. If some intended arrangement is not as visually appealing as you had hoped—and this will happen—then move the stakes to better convey what you had envisioned. Remember, though, to record all such adjustments as soon as possible on your basic study drawing in case you wish to review the layout further.

Once you have fully resolved a workable design package, including notations for the selected construction materials and plant sizes, you might do well to raise a few questions that you may have postponed in your initial zeal to find a productive design resolution. These questions relate to future maintenance. While any of us would certainly enjoy having an assortment of pleasurable garden additions, we have to recognize the maintenance effort and cost involved with their presence on the scene. For example, extensive lawn areas will need consistent and regular mowing; clipped hedges may demand more than just annual attention to look their best; lush perennial beds may require frequent division, refurbishing, and replanting; and reliable growth may necessitate a sprinkler system and frequent insect or disease spray programs.

All future maintenance chores should readily fit your lifestyle and budget since there is nothing more discouraging than seeing a stimulating design effort fail to live up to its full potential because of inadequate upkeep. The best approach is to organize the layout according to what you can readily manage without undue strain. After all, gardens are supposed to provide consistently satisfying comforts, not constant work and expense. The wise designer knows that simple effects done to perfection will always endure longer than elaborate ones handled with only puny aftercare.

Chapter 5

Unifying the Design

A unified design is one that suggests a single, coherent unit, whereby the various parts and colors in a composition have pleasurably blended into an agreeable and satisfactory statement of purpose. It promotes repose and serenity to an observer and is the most prized landscape quality because it shows the truest design artistry. Although you are unlikely to achieve a fully unified garden on the first try, you should continue to work toward it since it is the heart and soul of the entire enterprise. Leaving any loose ends or jarring visual combinations in place will never allow for a unified layout. All parts must come together convincingly. To guide us effectively toward this unified presentation, we have a trio of primary forms of design organization—repetition, sequence, and balance—and several design values—scale, proportion, emphasis, and rhythm—which are outlined in this chapter.

Design Principles of Order

The concepts of order in repetition, sequence, and balance—as well as in the design values—may seem equally fitting for compositions in painting, dance, or music, and because garden design is a high art form in its own right with a long and distinguished history (as you discovered in the first chapter of this book) the overlapping terminology is quite appropriate. Even today thousands of us trek across the globe to visit and admire the memorable handiwork of created gardens from many time periods and cultures. Who knows, perhaps one day your own garden development will become a must-see stopover, too. Consistently following the guidelines described here can be of substantial help to you—even if public showmanship is not your intended goal.

REPETITION

Probably the most fundamental and commonly used design principle is repetition, and it is quite simple to implement. All you need do is duplicate the same element in an orderly fashion as many times as you deem appropriate. Any same-plant hedge or garden-border edging is a perfect example of garden repetition. An equally spaced row of identical shade or flowering trees paralleling an entrance drive or property line also illustrates simple repetition while importantly knitting together the different areas of a landscape. Even a line of uniformly decorated pots or tubs neatly edging a paved or grassy terrace establishes repetition, provided that each element is equal in size, filled with similar plants, and equidistant in spacing.

This colorful sedum edging illustrates simple repetition.

Nevertheless, you risk drifting into monotony if you overdo any form of repetition beyond true design need. Some believe simplicity and repetition are equals, but in my view too much simplicity is just "playing it safe" and borders on dullness. When you provide little variation in your garden details, any uplifting pleasure initially gained from seeing them eventually fades to easy acceptance. We all benefit from attractive changes that produce visual stimulation from time to time.

The opposite of monotony is variety, which is too often described as "the spice of life." But just as too many spices can spoil a dinner, too many diversions of novel plant specimens or unusual garden artifacts can soon confuse and weary the mind of any viewer. Successful variety will offer meaningful contrasts with both a degree of pleasant surprise and distinctiveness. Typically, variety is not fulfilled just by stringing out a group of different plants or objects to occupy some empty space. Assembling a unified and compelling assortment of garden elements requires time and careful evaluation, which should also take into ac-

A repeated screen of ornamental pear (*Pyrus*) trees along a poolside property line is also an example of repetitive spacing.

count the specific location of every piece. Provide enough variety to stimulate the mind, yet not so much as to overwhelm it. There are times when less noticeability is a wiser path to follow.

SEQUENCE

Closely related to repetition is sequence, but it carries a somewhat different focus. While repetition is a succession of equal identities, sequence provides a break in the routine because it is the planned change in one characteristic—or two at the most—of a series. Its intent is to stimulate the eye to move in a special direction by noticeable yet subtle modification of the presented items. To illustrate, suppose you want your design to include a large bed of pink petunias but would prefer more visual interest than is offered by repeating one plant type and one color value throughout. If you divide this bed into parts, starting with pale pink and moving on to deep pink and concluding with dark pink, using equal numbers of each, you have made a sequential drift of graded pink flower interest.

Another common sequencing practice is to vary the leaf size of botanically related plants in a shrub bed. A display of evergreen hollies, for example, could

The formal placement of these Four Seasons statues offers a sequence of related poses.

start with the tiny foliage of the compact, ground-hugging Heller Japanese cultivar (*Ilex crenata* 'Helleri'), lead next to the taller and more wide-spreading mound of the Hetz Japanese cultivar (*I. crenata* 'Hetz') with its inch-long leaves, and then visually connect to a nearby pyramidally shaped and treelike English holly (*I. aquifolium*) showing 3-inch greenery. All carry equally glossy foliage, but the last one forms clusters of showy red fruit (on females) while the first two have nondescript black fruit—yet another sequential variation within the same framework.

Grouping garden statuary of the same size and material can fit this principle, too, when all the pieces have related presentations but dissimilar poses. A popular arrangement is the "Four Seasons" assembly, with either cherubs or young people offering different displays of flowers or fruit in fetching ways. Be watchful, however, that you do not introduce too many sequential changes just because the idea is intriguing, or you may lose the intended subtlety and special appeal that such variation offers.

BALANCE

The visual equilibrium of equal amounts of attraction is called balance. A symmetrical or formal balance (see also Chapter 3) produces a physically and visually identical layout on both sides of an axis, either vertical or horizontal. Asymmetric or informal balance combines dissimilar elements but still relates them along an axis. Either approach to achieving balance can appear from shapes, sizes, textures, or colorings promoted in the observed setting by either plants or artifacts.

Symmetric balance must be straightforwardly evident as soon as you enter a formal layout. Your attention here should easily and quickly shift from side to side in accepting the design's appropriateness. There should be no debate that any part is out of place, and one side should mirror the other exactly. Symmetrical planting is commonplace for many architectural styles throughout history, especially those that employ strict symmetry in a structure's front facade, such as regularly spaced, same-sized windows flanking a central doorway. The human body is itself physically balanced along a spinal axis, with the usual placement of duplicate arms, legs, eyes, and ears, and we relate comfortably to finding these formal similarities elsewhere, even if many people do not truly prefer that garden style today. Perhaps this mild rejection of overly formal presentation comes

Symmetric or formal balance is well illustrated here by both the construction elements and the planting details.

Asymmetric or informal balance is achieved by the careful assignment of plant masses and textures.

about because some see symmetric balance in a landscape as an obvious show-case for humanity's clever manipulations and therefore is not at all natural in effect.

This attitude may explain somewhat why the asymmetric or informal approach to garden design is now more popular than ever, and the many types of nonformal structures today from architects and builders undoubtedly have just as much influence here. When the front door of your house is offset you still need to maintain visual balance, and this irregularity encourages an asymmetric arrangement of the plant groupings. Whether you select one mix of evergreen and deciduous material or any other by personal interest, the selections for both sides of the main approach must represent a coordinated relationship of mass, texture, form, and color. Successful planting balance using either formal or informal design will come to pass once you carefully determine how to blend your house style and its setting seamlessly for the visual benefit of both.

Design Values

A design value is the relative worth or degree of importance derived from the use of various elements in a composition. These are most clearly expressed by the terms scale, proportion, emphasis, and rhythm, and each value interacts with another in a subtle or dramatic fashion depending upon your personal choices. Whether used in complex or very simple ways, design values are key ingredients to understanding how to gain a higher artistic result.

SCALE

Simply put, scale is the relative size of any object as compared with another. People themselves are the useful means by which all sense of proper scale is measured in judging whether something is too large, too small, or "just right" for inclusion in a setting. Determining the correct size of an object mainly comes to us from past experiences and judgments. We all make size comparisons in our daily lives, and the more variations we evaluate in depth, the more we are quickly able to differentiate their characteristics of scale.

In a home landscape, the dimensions, layout, and volume of the house, along with all existing large trees spread throughout the property, readily establish a primary scale that your intended adjacent garden developments need to complement well, or else the layouts will seem puny. All new planting additions, plus such major construction improvements as a terrace, wall, fence, or entry walk, must reflect correct proportions of scale within this basic framework. Of course, the majority of us can hardly afford to bring in a complete array of mature plant specimens immediately for a finished landscape effect, so we are usually forced to install smaller sizes and then wait for future growth to complete the intended picture.

One oddity of garden design work is that while any architectural element—terrace, walk, fence, gazebo, or pool—is presented to us in a fully completed form ready for immediate use, the planting aspect normally has to cope with many out-of-scale outlines and skinny volumes for the first few years. Those paltry sticks of new shrubs will eventually fulfill their promises, and the sad-looking clumps of starter perennials will enlarge to catalog-like lushness, but it is difficult to believe with such a chancy start that anything worthwhile will happen in our lifetimes.

But happen it will, so space all key material properly to provide ample room now for normal stretching up and out later. Gardens are man-made treats for the eye and the spirit, but because all our new plantings are put in place by our insistence and direction, we really have no one to blame but ourselves when plants grow out of scale for their locations and then require complete removal and a renewal planting installed with more promise for the future. All garden material ages to dimensions different from the initial planting size, modifying the space it inhabits by its expansion. Even with frequent—or just occasional—neatness pruning, some plants will always dominate at the expense of timid-growing companions, so it is wise to understand a plant's behavior from the start. Time will bring changes.

With plants, scale is not just related to the ultimate height and spread but also to the natural branching structure and leaf proportions. The husky limbs and broad, star-shaped foliage of a sycamore (*Platanus*), for example, harmonize more easily with nearby large-leaved rhododendrons of ample girth than with the dainty, inch-long leaves and pencil-thin stems of barberry (*Berberis*). The space occupied by a bed of any repeated shrub, ground cover, or vine also affects the scale of a setting and its acceptability for a viewer. Such understory bedding is more visually effective when its outer dimensions stretch at least to the farthest limits of the branching of any tree or group of trees within that

Out-of-scale planting can obscure important house features.

Correctly scaled new planting and construction now reveals the full attractiveness of the house and setting.

bed. Collaring independently set trees with a narrow doily of summer annuals (a common favorite), spring bulbs, or even perennials is totally out of scale and visually distracting. It compares to a hippopotamus with an ankle bracelet, and no garden setting deserves such an oddity.

PROPORTION

With outdoor designs, proportion refers to the relative distribution of the elements used. This concept dictates just how many different shapes, sizes, colors, and textures can be comfortably accommodated in an area before a sense of clutter sets in. Both planting and construction are involved in the creation of visual acceptability here. Too many differently colored or variably textured building materials viewed together are just as difficult to accept as a hodgepodge of unrelated plant types colliding with each other. Instead, the design should be subtle, allowing just a few main items to dominate while other related parts assume subsidiary or helper roles.

Proportions enter into all details of garden creation. The heft of a masonry pier constructed from stone or brick at a drive entry can look peculiarly inharmonious, for example, if any decorative stonework or light fixture is too

Lost in the haphazardness of the planting, the spotty rocks and color dabs contribute little value to this setting.

diminutive or oversized for such a support base. Brick or stone walks and terraces should be laid tightly butted together, or with no more than a half-inch
joint of mortar or sand, to allow the construction pieces to have primary interest, not the repetitive seams that hold the work together. One way to further reduce the noticeability of masonry joints is to darken the mortar with lampblack
or use sand or stone grit in deep tones.

In nature, plants seem to appear in great quantities of the same type
bunched together in colonies. This bounty helps promote reliable fertilization
for the next generation, but the effect is often more appreciated for its showy appeal to the eye. Copy this technique for garden planting, especially with hardy
bulbs since they always look more attractive when massed. This arrangement
concentrates color value and allows for some cut-flower collecting without
major disturbance to the garden display. Stringing bulbs out in a soldierly fash-

This subtle Oriental composition has proper proportions of rock and planting, with the
boulder and other rocks emphasized for their garden value and complemented by the
subdued, textural plantings.

A carved stone finial placed on a proportionately scaled base.

Framing shade trees supply emphasis for an entry driveway.

ion of rigid lines along the front of a border is visually weak and ineffective. If you experience some blooming failure, or even pick a few blossoms for a bouquet, you end up with a "missing-tooth" look of little value. There is safety in numbers, and proper proportions throughout a garden determine just how successful any space becomes.

EMPHASIS

A sense of forceful significance is the hallmark of emphasis, and it is a useful means for deliberately directing attention. A tunneling archway of large-scaled shade or evergreen trees lining both sides of an entry drive focuses attention—and even heightens anticipation—toward arrival at the house. By flanking a major opening in a hedge with tall, matched, spiky, needled evergreens (or columnar, deciduous trees) you intrigue the eye and tantalize the mind with the suggestion that a different garden atmosphere may unfold once you pass through this gateway. Here you may come upon a sunken garden with a splashing pool jet, a fragrant rose collection, or whatever unexpected but stimulating change from the previous location. Those sentry evergreens simply provide a silent but compelling emphasis announcing your discovery route.

Because emphasis can supply significant garden drama, you should be careful about overextending its use. Limit it only to those features that are truly important since too many emphatic repetitions can create a restlessness that suggests indecision about which parts of the design have greatest significance.

RHYTHM

When any line or sequence of a composition is broken repeatedly at equal intervals, you create pulsing alterations that give the sensation of rhythm. In musical arrangements this effect is defined as the cadence or the beat, and in garden layouts rhythm offers the same type of nonrandom contrasts of strong and weak elements. These intervals can be presented by form, pattern, or color value and are designed to carry your eye comfortably across the whole layout. This design value may at first appear to be quite similar to the principle of repetition detailed earlier, but it noticeably differs in that rhythm is the deliberate separation of nonidentical, but closely related, elements along a range of fixed distances. Rhythm, then, is created by interruptions of variable action, whereas repetition reflects both continuity and identicalness.

A technique of rhythm in design that involves construction elements can be illustrated by a streetside fence line of horizontal wood rails and upright posts all painted the same color. If located in a very sunny location, the design can be embellished by adding a single climbing rose in a red tone to each of the odd-numbered posts and a pink climbing rose to each even-numbered post. Now you have produced a rhythm of similar-textured, same-blooming plants with a repeated color change set out at regular intervals. Plants grouped for a rhythmic end need to maintain similar masses, textures, and blooming periods to be most effective. If the plant types on this fence were to flower at distinctly different times, leaving one set in just foliage, then you have a stronger sense of repetition than rhythm.

In a more complex example, let us arrange a flower border atop a stone wall that encloses a family sitting area. This rhythmic design will feature tall snapdragons in two colors distributed throughout two equal beds 44 feet long set at right angles to each other. Each bed is 4 feet wide and exposed to roughly the same amount of daily sunlight. Start with a 2-foot setback from one end of a border and install twelve white snapdragons (each plant here is 6 inches on center from its neighbor) three parallel rows deep. Four more feet along, set out a block of twelve yellow snapdragons also three rows deep. Repeat this pattern every 4 feet so that you end with a block of white snapdragons on both ends. These snapdragons create a rhythmic pattern of their own. Next, flank each side of both the white and the yellow snapdragons with a dozen blue ageratum and complete the background by planting nine medium-height, pale yellow marigolds in each of the remaining open areas between the ageratum. Since there should be a foot of available frontage left, finish by edging the whole arrangement with very low, pale yellow marigolds (white sweet alyssum is a workable alternative here). You have now produced a rhythmic pattern of summer annuals with related color values and flower forms.

At the beginning of this chapter you read that unity is the successful blending of all garden elements—plants, construction, and artifacts—into a visually satisfying whole. When unity is achieved, a landscape composition of any style will offer a three-dimensional expression of pictorial cohesiveness worthy of attention. Your own skill in formulating such a result will improve markedly as you continue to use all the design aids provided here.

This rhythmic border of summer annuals uses color variations within the same plant types.

A cohesive, unified garden space.

Should you feel overly challenged by extensive garden making, however, or find that you have less ability or time to pursue your ideas to a successful conclusion, do not hesitate to enlist the aid of a professional to guide your efforts along. The majority of licensed landscape architects, garden designers, and planting specialists include as part of their daily schedules paid consultation about garden design problems. Each can likely provide another point of view and a program to suit your gardening aims and projected budget. Employed early in the proceedings, such outside guidance can also provide substantial savings of time and effort. When in doubt, seek help. Paying for sound, intelligent advice likely will save you money in the end.

Chapter 6

—

The Stimulus of Color

The color choices employed throughout your garden development can make all the difference between calmness and chaos, since color is a key element in motivating greater reaction to what you see, and our eyes notice color before we recognize an object's shape. Someone once said that it might be better to think in black and white when laying out a design because having color at the start could distract you from recognizing any flaws in the composition. Yet garden color is always present and belongs importantly in your evaluation of the total picture you are creating. Take away all color from a scene and you are left with either pitch blackness or dazzling whiteness, situations carrying either no light reflection or the fullness of all available light. Color is mainly concerned with light, as you will soon learn when you read on.

Color Fundamentals

All objects reflect light in various intensities according to the basic structure of their pigments as well as their surface textures. You surely have observed that a smoothly polished finish reflects much more light than a rough, weather-beaten one. Fuzzy foliage also absorbs more light than glossy foliage does. Dark colors hold more light than bright ones, and light reflected on an object can alter its apparent color. We therefore have several types of color fundamentals to evaluate: the pigments within objects, the texture of all the surfaces involved, and the color of the light itself. Put all three together and you get the actual color you see.

Yet the color identified with an object is never static since it changes with the hours of the day and the seasons of the year, primarily by the alterations in the intensity of light. Even passing clouds act as filters, diluting light intensity from the sun and therefore altering the color values we see from moment to moment. Every experienced garden photographer is familiar with the effect—and frustration—of these changing outdoor circumstances when attempting to capture the "true" color of a plant or garden scene.

The Color Wheel

Most people first become acquainted with the fundamental color wheel in childhood. Greek mythology tells of the rainbow messenger, Iris, bringing color as a special gift to humanity to brighten our lives. What people experienced visually before that delightful present is mystifyingly unclear, but at least we have color twenty-four hours a day now.

Pigments and light use the same elementary color range found in the wedge-divided circle known as the spectrum. First we have the primary colors of red, yellow, and blue, called primary because all other colors can be made from mixing them together in some proportion or another. Between the primaries in the color wheel are the secondary colors of orange, green, and violet, and each of these is a blend of two primary colors. Placed side by side, each primary color has enormous intensity, but the effect is much less assertive in comparison to a neighboring secondary color because the two colors share a common pigment association.

For landscape use, some subtly satisfying color combinations can readily be arranged by using a concept called the *harmony of triads*. Here, three related color values are assembled in different proportions both to suit your personal preferences and to blend well with existing colors from plants, structures, or artifacts. A workable arrangement is to pair two of the colors for emphasis and place the third for accent interest. Using the primary colors of red, yellow, and blue—translated to the landscape tones of russet, citron, and slate, for example—creates an initial harmony of triads. Combine both russet and citron for the main emphasis here with slate as the accent, which could be a container or even a bench color. For the secondary color range of orange, green, and violet, landscape substitutions include buff, sage, and plum. In this instance, buff and plum could be the emphasis with sage the accent, probably as a foliage coloring. The question of which color value serves as the accent is a personal matter. Other tonal variations are possible, of course, since outdoor color values are wide-ranging and intriguing.

Garden schemes that are predominately yellow always seem welcoming and attractive, especially with an intermingling of white or creamy accents. Perhaps this is because they effectively combine the well-appreciated color values of bright sun and fluffy clouds on a summer's day. Blue flowers, by contrast, may

This yellow-focused garden invites casual strolling.

appear dull and somewhat drab since blue surfaces absorb most of the open light striking them without much reflection. To perk up blue elements add a dash of pale yellow, strong purple, or an occasional orange accent, plus spurts of gray foliage.

Red and purple flower groups cooperate harmoniously when interlaced with pink additions and just a touch of white. In addition, gray rock walls or exposed ledge formations, along with dark green to gray-green evergreen backgrounds, are often nicely enlivened by violet, purple, or pink flower displays near them. Simple and subtle color presentations can even be arranged from using just the contrasting and variable tones of green foliage of deciduous plants. Any contrast of colorings can be stimulating since such juxtapositions highlight recognizable color relationships without overwhelming either contributor. Proper blending is the watchword.

The color chart is designed as a wheel of six wedge-shaped spokes, and each color is located diagonally opposite its complementary color. Yellow and violet, for example, are opposite, indicating that each will gain in intensity when used

Red and purple salvias mix harmoniously with pink and white ones.

together. The same is true for red and green as well as blue and orange. Intriguingly, these basic color associations have long histories of identification with common Western celebrations: yellow and violet for Easter, red and green for Christmas, and—stretching a bit—very deep blue, modified to black, and orange for Halloween. No doubt people of earlier history made these connections by observing the natural color values in the seasonal changes of the plant life around them and used these combinations to mark special occasions. Color really does create some long-lasting human memories.

Dimensions of Color

Color has three main dimensions: hue, value, and intensity. Hue is the name of a color. The value describes whether it is lighter in tone, now called a tint, or darker than the parent hue and renamed a shade. The intensity of any color is the concentrated strength—orange, for example, is a high-intensity color while apricot has a lower intensity value. These three dimensions are importantly interlocked so that changing one aspect will force some adjustment to another. When you dilute, or tint, a hue, you also thin out its intensity as well.

While we can easily alter paint or dye pigments by adding either black or white (along with a mix of these called gray) for additional, intermediate values, when it comes to plant material for garden use we are forced to work with only the colors currently available in the nurseries. No matter who we are we cannot demand new colors on a whim, and therefore we need to be clever with the color palette that exists at the moment. The list of color selections is hardly a minor one, however, since plant breeders and nurseries are constantly bringing new color improvements of flowers, foliage, and fruit every year.

The Color of Light

The natural color of light has a major effect on the pigment coloring of the objects it strikes since light is either absorbed or reflected to some degree by all surfaces. We have all endured the experience of suddenly coming upon a brilliantly lit white wall at noon. We quickly squint our eyes nearly shut as the full intensity of the sun is reflected back at us with the total spectrum of available light in its pure white form. Any dark-toned object in this scene absorbs some of the shimmering noontime brilliance and thus appears duller than any bright object nearby. During such eye-wearying experiences all color values seem "washed out." Contrast this same view an hour or so after dawn or just before sunset and these same colors will appear far different. Pastels observed in noon brightness will be very faint, but at dawn or dusk these highly reflective colorings will stand out more, especially white or pale yellow. By twilight all light-absorbing blue or red flowers, along with deep green foliage, practically disappear from view, while the same white or yellow accents will retain much of their reflective appeal even in the encroaching dimness.

The changing angle of the sun over the seasons, the type of cloud cover filtering the sun's intensity, and the particular time of day each significantly affect the color of light reaching outdoor objects. Sunlight, then, is one garden influence over which we have no jurisdiction, except to modify its intensity.

Adjusting Light Intensity

Adjusting the intensity of sunlight can be accomplished in several simple ways. You can readily reduce the strength of natural light by having it filter through the foliage of tall trees before shining on the garden. Deciduous trees are better than evergreens for this purpose since they not only grow proportionately faster but also allow different degrees of light to penetrate to the ground in each season. Additionally, you can influence the type of surface that catches the light. If you require more brightness in an area, add shiny surfaces such as polished stones or plants with waxy foliage, such as is offered by most evergreen hollies. Where a dulling down of reflections is preferable, incorporate clumps of light-absorbing, fuzzy foliage, like that of perennial wormwood (*Artemisia*), or use the light-mutating characteristics of weathered-timber furniture or fencing. Deeper colored outdoor furniture also reduces glare, especially when painted with flat finishes, and black makes any garden object far less noticeable, if that is your goal.

Effects of Color

At some point in history the term "warm" was assigned to describe red, orange, and yellow—the colors readily observed in the sun's changing appearance from

Tall deciduous trees create shadows that effectively filter intense sunlight.

Light-colored tree bark and shrub foliage aids in visually enlarging an area.

dawn to dusk—while blue, green, and violet are called "cool" colorings because they remind us of water bodies, deep woods, and shadows. Warm colors also appear to advance toward us, but the cool ones tend to withdraw, which provides us with a useful way to make a space seem smaller or larger by tricking the eye through color placement. White or pale yellow seen at a distance often visually enlarge a scene, especially if used in quantity.

Nevertheless, the greater visual vitality of the warm colors tend to be so emotionally exciting to us that their overuse can actually bring on mental strain and even irritation at times. Limpid or cool colorings on the other hand are valued for their soothing and relaxing qualities, yet even they can leave you feeling dull and dispirited if excessively dominating. Color does indeed influence our moods, and the mix that we select can offer a variety of stimulations.

Seasonal Color in Plants

Although green is the dominant color in plant foliage, it naturally alters with the seasons. What may have first appeared in spring as frail, translucent, mostly yellow-green new growth (especially with deciduous material) becomes thicker, opaque, and deeper toned by summer. Native spring flowers usually range from white to creamy yellow or from pale pink to lavender, but by summertime any new floral displays from Nature tend to take on rich tones of red, orange, deep yellow, bright blue, and purple. (Nursery introductions are another matter and rarely stay within color bounds at any season.)

A garden space that in early summer has a varied mix of plants heralding the season by autumn can have an entirely altered visual effect with the arrival of vivid changes in foliage on deciduous trees and shrubs, which have been carefully selected beforehand to provide this desirable transformation. For several weeks, a totally new look of garden interest is achieved as the entire outline of a shrub or tree glows with extensive color. Even brown tones are more acceptable in this season.

During the winter resting period you can produce additional color appeal by incorporating trees such as birch (*Betula*), crape myrtle (*Lagerstroemia*), or eucalyptus that display mottled or flaking bark on trunks and branches. Heavy clusters of durable fruit, as found on crabapple (*Malus*) and holly (*Ilex*), also brighten wintertime doldrums, as do the colorful red or yellow stems of several

A mix of summertime flower and leaf colorings along a garden path.

The same view in autumn offers foliage attractions from deciduous plants.

shrub dogwoods (*Cornus*). The silhouettes of specimen plants offer scenic value, too, particularly those of husky evergreens such as pine (*Pinus*) and spruce (*Picea*) set against open sky.

Of course, the employment of color in a successful garden layout extends beyond plant choices. The hues expressed by structures, walkways, fencing, walls, statuary, and even outdoor furniture must harmonize appropriately, too. No item can be left to chance if you want to achieve superior color blending. Whether used for its boldness or its delicateness, color is an invaluable tool that we should employ wisely and correctly. After all, it is a gift from the gods.

Winter snow dramatizes both evergreen and deciduous silhouettes.

Chapter 7

Evergreen Plant Considerations

Our planet is crowded with intriguing plants of every description, many of which we find useful for transferring to gardens. Although a sizable number of the woody ones are evergreen, the majority still appears to be deciduous or annual leaf-shedding sorts, and both of these main categories contribute a magnificent range of forms and sizes. Then there are the extensive annuals, perennials, bulbs, ferns, and grasses for carpeting the lower ground level. We have a wide assortment of vegetation from which to pick and choose for our garden use. Let us begin with an investigation of the evergreens.

An evergreen is defined here as a woody plant that persistently holds its normally green foliage throughout the year in eye-pleasing condition, even when dormant or resting. In colder areas this period of nongrowth also allows for the maintenance of durable and attractive greenery through persistent frosts and icy winds. Because of this year-long leafy effect, both needle and broadleaf evergreens make invaluable landscape contributions to the majority of our garden designs. They define any space enclosure with consistent greenery, provide wind and view restrictions, add solid bulk, serve effectively as dense backdrops for foreground displays, and create showy specimens throughout the year. It is little wonder, then, that evergreens are often called "the aristocrats" of the plant world.

Evergreen plants are more costly to buy than deciduous ones because they require transplanting with a sizable ball of earth around them to maintain an adequate source of soil moisture for their volume of persistent foliage. Sturdy as they may appear, evergreens have somewhat fragile root systems that resent rough handling and any substantial drying-out of the earth ball during the moving process. Regular and adequate follow-through watering is also necessary once they are replanted. Expect less growth in the first season following transplanting as the plant regrows its feeder roots, many of which were necessarily severed at the nursery.

Evergreens are usually slower growing compared to the majority of deciduous plants. They are readily distinguished by their well-defined silhouettes and heavy foliage masses throughout the seasons. Every growing area of the globe has native types with some useful garden appeal, yet many introduced kinds have also adapted well to nonnative homes, thus greatly extending our plant diversity. All evergreens, whether needled or broad-leaved, are basically considered rich in appearance as foliage accents, and those with conspicuous flowering are even richer. Insofar as we now know, no needle evergreen vines are out there to investigate for garden use.

Uncrowded pines keep their lower branches for longer periods.

Representative needle evergreens are usually coniferous, or cone-bearing, but a few of these conifers are oddly not evergreen. For example, the larch (*Larix*) has cones but completely sheds its needle crop annually. This tree is sometimes jokingly, but inaccurately, described as a "deciduous evergreen," but it is just a nonconforming member of a large plant group, where exceptions are obviously possible.

Useful as evergreens may be for year-round screening purposes, totally evergreen layouts tend to become dark, overpowering, and even gloomy as they mature. The needled tree forms such as pine, spruce, or fir, which can stretch upward to 100 feet or more, throw very long shadows, adding to the dimness of their surroundings. Small garden areas, specifically, should not be overplanted with such tall evergreens. Mixing evergreens with various deciduous trees, however, can lighten the effect, especially with plants offering showy blooms, colorful fruit, or vivid autumn foliage. A skillful designer will recognize early the visual benefits of incorporating a variety of plant contrasts within any garden scene.

Needle Evergreen Trees and Shrubs

Trees and shrubs in the needle evergreen category have silhouettes that are normally dense and cast solid shadows, yet their individual needles can be either fine and slender, as in hemlock (*Tsuga*), pine (*Pinus*), and fir (*Abies*), or else scale-like and flattened, as seen on arborvitae (*Thuja*), juniper (*Juniperus*), and cypress (*Cupressus* or *Chamaecyparis*). The tree forms have dominant, upright, broad outlines and usually deep green foliage, yet special types also offer new growth in gray, silver, blue, bronze, and yellow alternatives either as natural hybrids or as nursery selections. On the whole these tree types have single, hefty trunks supporting many close layers of either horizontal or drooping branches right down to ground level—at least when not overcrowded or deeply shaded by other nearby plants, which can cause a thinning of the bottom branching.

In contrast, the needle evergreen shrubs usually produce many main stems with either spreading, creeping, or upright habits. The shrubs also offer color variations, and the spreading forms are often installed to create interwoven mats of foliage with no distinguishing separation of the individual units. The lowest-growing forms, particularly the junipers, are truly ground covers of evergreen distinction.

Both the needled trees and shrubs present widely variable outlines and textures well suited for many garden uses. As a group they adapt better to windy sites than do the broadleaf forms, due to the small surfaces of their narrow leaves. This protection against wind damage is further aided by a coating of natural wax called cutin, which occurs mainly on the top of the leaf. The gloss is not as prominent as that on broadleaf plants, but it still performs its job well.

Dwarf Conifers

Within the wide range of available plant choices, several hundred dwarf conifers provide unique landscape appeal—and a fascinating history. These special plants are needle evergreens miniaturized in all their parts (although some will achieve moderately large size after a long time) and are usually so slow that an annual expansion of one inch is considered vigorous. These pygmy forms are called mutants or sports, indicating that the particular plant has radically departed from its parents' characteristics in some major way. Such dwarfs are unable to pass along their special attributes, however, unless they are propagated by stem cuttings.

Shrub junipers are available in a wide variety of forms and colors.

Cone production is rare, and if any seeds were produced, their germinated growth would likely further diversify the specific plant type. Because of the long time and effort required to produce a large supply of landscape-size dwarf conifers, these unusual plants are relatively expensive in the nursery trade.

Dwarf conifers are also very difficult to locate in wild forests—at least *in* the earth. The majority appear, instead, at noticeably deformed branch tips of various needle evergreen trees, mostly high up in the tree crowns. Reaching these stunted growths is no simple matter, and since they have no independent roots, they must be pruned off the parent. Collecting new types is undoubtedly a memorable experience.

We now believe that the dwarf forms mainly originate when leaf buds on parent trees become infected with a virus disorder called *hexenbesen,* or "witches broom" disease, spread by foraging insects. The damaged growth resulting in the dwarf conifer has the same coloring and needle arrangement as the parent, but its habit is greatly reduced and can range from upright to spreading depending upon the character of the parent. Occasionally these dwarfs in garden use show some later reversion to the larger parent by sending out an elongated

A border of dwarf Hinoki cypress (*Chamaecyparis obtusa* 'Nana') used as an informal hedge.

shoot, and this should be promptly cut off, or else the plant could become a real oddity.

Dwarf conifers currently have wide garden appeal for many locations not only because they are slow growing but because of their unusual diversity. Their extremely simple maintenance involves no trimming except to remove aberrant shoots, some balanced fertilizer once each spring, and a good soaking during drought. Used individually, as a hedge line, or in a mixed collection, the dwarf conifer offers distinction for any garden where it will succeed. Nursery availability has grown quite impressively, even if the plants themselves do not.

Broadleaf Evergreen Trees, Shrubs, and Vines

By the simplest of definitions, a broadleaf evergreen has persistent foliage wider and longer than that of any needled type, and this leaf size varies considerably within the group, from the quarter-inch greenery of shrub box (*Buxus*) and dwarf holly (*Ilex*) to the almost 8-inch leaf blades found on rosebay rhododendron (*Rhododendron maximum*) and southern magnolia. Some forms, such as the 'PJM' dwarf rhododendron cultivar, even change their green summer foliage into mahogany or other reddish tones for the entire winter dormancy, and this color is more strongly developed when the plant is grown in full sun.

For added garden pleasure, many broadleaf evergreens flower conspicuously, such as mountain laurel (*Kalmia*), azalea, camellia, and oleander (*Nerium*), or produce showy and durable fruit displays, as seen commonly with pyracantha, nandina, and most hollies (*Ilex*). As you might expect, a few oddities are also found here, such as the ground-hugging heath (*Erica*) and heather (*Calluna*) with their long-lasting flower spikes and needlelike foliage. Such blossoming and subsequent seed capsules separate them from the cone-bearing evergreens even though their appearance when not in bloom certainly makes it seem as if heath and heather belong there.

Popular creeping and climbing evergreen vines such as English ivy (*Hedera*), euonymus, jasmine (*Jasminum*), and creeping fig (*Ficus*), together with the mat-forming ground covers myrtle (*Vinca*), pachysandra, and lilyturf (*Liriope*), are also important contributors to this broadleaf assembly.

Broadleaf evergreens normally have shallow, fibrous root systems and a conspicuously shiny coating of waxy cutin on the upper sides of their leaves. Appealingly variegated or at least differently toned foliage on certain forms of creeping euonymus as well as on English holly (*Ilex aquifolium*) offer an appealing, subtle contrast with any nearby plain-green plantings. The variegated leaves lack a complete dose of chlorophyll, and so the foliage may also be somewhat less resistant to wind or ice damage in the dormant season, even if the plant itself is hardy under those conditions.

Many broadleaf evergreens, especially the sizable rhododendron group, adapt better than the needled forms to lower light intensity, such as when shaded by nearby large trees or structures. The broadleaf foliage, however, often becomes elongated, thinner, and oddly glossier under these conditions. Any flower production may be reduced and the coloring less intense as compared to that on similar plants growing in stronger light.

As a group the broadleaf evergreens dislike constant drying or icy winds and can show appreciable leaf-edge browning annually when these conditions persist year after year. They also resent prolonged drought, and some types, such as rhododendrons, express their displeasure with drooping, curled foli-

The all-green foliage of rosebay rhododendron (*Rhododendron maximum*) is effectively fronted with a bed of yellow-toned creeping euonymus (*Euonymus fortunei* 'Emerald 'n' Gold').

age, which requires quick and thorough watering relief. Because most of their roots remain closely set at the upper soil surface, the broadleaf evergreens exhibit greater growth response when consistently mulched with a moisture-retentive, organic root cover at all times. Cultivating in their surface root zone is detrimental and is unneeded with mulching.

Palms

Exhibiting enormous diversity with thousands of identified species, palms are unique, normally sun-loving broad-leaved trees adaptable to a surprisingly wide range of geographic locales. Closely related botanically to the grass family, palms are unusual for their often simple but bold silhouettes. They carry widely expansive, split leaves called fronds and a topmost growth bud, which if severely damaged by frost or other causes will bring about withering or even death to the entire plant.

Palms contribute a diversity of forms and color shadings.

An impressive clustering of older California Washingtonia palms.

Most of us picture palms only as very tall evergreens with unbranched trunks and a coconut-like fruit suitable for humid, tropical or subtropical areas—and the majority do thrive natively in such surroundings—but their full identity goes well beyond these climate zones and typical silhouettes. Palms are remarkably far-ranging in adaptability and quite diverse in form, including even somewhat shrublike types. Many are multistemmed with squat outlines, while others are truly dwarfed and are well suited to small gardens and outdoor containers. When it comes to cold tolerance, a select few adapt well to the lowland parts of zone 8, areas not usually thought of as typical palm country.

Compared to other broadleaf evergreens, the root system of palms is curious since only the short-lived, unbranched tips make any growth extensions to collect soil water and then never much enlarge in thickness. Transplants require a very well drained site and generous follow-through watering on a regular basis until the plants are fully established. Very tall transplanted specimens may require sturdy wood bracing or hefty guy wires to keep them from toppling in strong winds before their roots are fully established in the soil, which may take more than a year.

Any pruning need for palms is minimal and normally consists of cutting away dead fronds both for appearance and for the inherent fire hazard presented by these bone-dry leaves. The repeated clean-up of dropped, mushy fruit from some types is more of a maintenance problem, however, so be sure to install the known messy kinds well away from main walks, driveways, terraces, and swimming pools.

Chapter 8

Deciduous and Herbaceous Plant Considerations

Deciduous Trees, Shrubs, and Vines

By far the largest number of nursery-available trees, shrubs, and woody vines are in the deciduous or annual leaf-shedding category. So many, in fact, that growers and mail-order companies offer only a small fraction of what exists for garden use. This plant group is hugely varied as to size, outline, coloring, leaf shape, and blooming sequence, offering more choices than the entire evergreen list. Every year a large number of deciduous woody plants are hybridized by growers seeking improved flower, fruit, or foliage traits for the simple reason that deciduous plants propagate more easily and grow to salable size faster than most evergreens.

With generally more resilient root systems than evergreens, a number of small, deciduous plants (roses are a striking example) can be shipped quite safely without any earth cover. Landscape-size deciduous plants normally prefer a sizable accompanying ball of earth for transplanting, but this is often done more for greater anchoring at the new location than for any horticultural need. In the many decades before the invention of the motorized hauling equipment commonly used today, even 40-foot shade trees were lugged bare-rooted, wrapped just in wet burlap shrouds, by teams of straining horses, and the plants not only survived this treatment but usually thrived afterward. Of course, this bare-root method of planting then required a large number of guy wires, perhaps for several years, to secure the trees against blowing over. Today's methods for transplanting are more efficient, but they are not really much different.

Deciduous plants accept more severe pruning than the majority of evergreens, and they recover more quickly with generous new growth in a short time. For example, an established but overgrown deciduous lilac (*Syringa*) shrub, or the related privet (*Ligustrum*), can be thinned of extraneous branches or even cut back almost to ground level every decade over its lifetime without apparent harm. This regular removal of older stems from many deciduous plants is a common method of rejuvenating the selection for greater flower and fruit response later. Such pruning treatment also contributes better air circulation to forestall the spread of some diseases as well as to improve the overall silhouette. Harsh shaping normally should be followed by a generous dose of appropriate fertilizer and adequate watering during the growing season to hasten the new, fill-in growth.

The majority of deciduous plants climax the end of their growing season with a showy bonus of strikingly colorful autumnal foliage changes along with potential crops of plentiful, late-summer fruiting that is attractive to a variety of wildlife. Because of the leaf loss over the long winter months, deciduous plants may be unwise choices for screening or other situations where greater privacy is

A dense screen of common lilac (*Syringa vulgaris*) has impressive blooming.

Showy autumnal foliage changes appear from a wide variety of deciduous plants.

Deciduous holly (*Ilex*) cultivars develop generous quantities of shiny, durable fruit.

desired. Substituting or blending in evergreens is a common resolution for this problem, but it is better if you understand your site needs well before this extra effort is required.

Deciduous vines in search of strong light are often vigorous growers and can quickly climb to the tops of nearby trees and shrubs, smothering the natural outlines of these support plants, often to an unattractive effect. Bittersweet (*Celastrus*) and wisteria are common examples of vines that exhibit rampant growth, and both can quickly encircle the host's branches so tightly as to cause die-back or even complete strangulation. Other deciduous vines, such as clematis and woodbine (*Parthenocissus*), however, show more refined growth habits and can provide attractive accents of seasonal flowering or autumn foliage color, without any harm to the supporting host shrub or tree.

The high-reaching woodbine (*Parthenocissus*) offers attractive autumn coloring and will not harm support trees or shrubs.

Cactuses

Cactuses are long-lived, fleshy perennials with either woody or herbaceous, blue-green to all-green, ribbed stems laden with chlorophyll. In place of foliage, cactuses form unique clusters of sharp spines, scales, or long hairs, offering an odd but fascinating array of distinct silhouettes. While the typical cactus is either round or candle-like in form, other natural sorts resemble barrels, eggs, pancakes, or mounds. A special few even have stems that lay prostrate and appear to crawl as they expand. Heights vary from an impressive 50 feet to a lowly 12 inches, with comparable but variable spreads.

Colorful flowers normally appear generously along or atop these chunky stems in the winter season and can be boldly dramatic and large or more modest and diminutive, yet all will certainly be noticeable. Fleshy, edible fruit suitable for human enjoyment develops over a long period on a few types, though the bulk of these juicy attractions are consumed by local wildlife.

A collection of unusual cactus forms.

Native almost exclusively to the Americas, these unusual plants were totally unknown to Europeans until the voyages of discovery and conquest in the sixteenth century. Cactuses are mostly sun-loving plants that inhabit the open deserts and semideserts of the western and southwestern United States, occurring naturally where summers are consistently hot and very dry, with yearly rainfall never exceeding one foot. With their roots located close to the surface, these plants resent any cultivation, and they insist on quick soil drainage at all times or else will begin to rot.

Gardens that display just cactuses are rare and usually appear a bit awkward. A more common practice is to combine them sympathetically with other native succulents and dry-season material into informally arranged desert scenes, complete with large boulders and smaller rocks and with the entire setting knitted together with a stone mulch. Such garden designs can create a distinctive and much admired landscape attraction if appropriately harmonized with the surroundings.

Several cactuses, such as this tuna species (*Opuntia*), display sizable and edible fruit.

Herbaceous Perennials, Bulbs, Ferns, Ornamental Grasses, and Annuals

Without a doubt the largest sequence of sustained color production and textural interest for the average garden space will come from using the wealth of ground-level support plants represented by the popular herbaceous perennials, bulbs, ferns, ornamental grasses, and annuals. Hundreds of different sorts in each category are available from a wide variety of sources, and you can count on seeing new introductions every year. The scope of this list of desirable garden material makes the selection process both exhilarating and a bit daunting, but at least the cost factors are reasonable enough to allow experimentation without breaking the budget.

The perennial selections range in size from the inch-high fuzz of the moss sandwort (*Arenaria*) to the 10-foot stalks of pampas grass (*Cortaderia*). Perennials also encompass such well-known bulbs as tulips and lilies. Widely available

Begonia, geranium, and grape ivy (*Cissus*) thriving in a decorative garden pot.

through nurseries or mail-order firms, a range of durable perennials are suitable for every type of soil, hardiness zone, rainfall, wind exposure, sunlight, and blossoming time. The rainbow world of annuals assists in breaching the gap of color continuity as the perennials pass their flowering prime, and they also fill in attractively at spots where spring bulbs once held sway. Many annuals adapt with ease to the confinement of a window box or a decorative garden pot. Herbaceous perennials and summer annuals belong together in gardens.

Because of their welcome endurance over many years—often decades—plus their ready acceptance of division and subdivision to create more plants, perennials are genuine mainstays of gardeners everywhere. As illustrated by the hundreds of hardy types described and pictured in my *Gardening with Perennials Month by Month* (Timber Press, 1993), designers in every growing area can readily assemble a remarkable assortment of on-going blossom displays and textural contrasts. Since that book offers no specific planting layouts, I will present a few suggestions here for making a typical design with blooming effects lasting from spring into autumn.

A few simple rules apply for getting the best response and appearance out of your perennials. First, for a mixed bed select only those plants that are equally well suited to the same conditions of light and soil moisture. Of course, each plant also needs to be reliably hardy for your growing area and readily adaptable to the appropriate soil pH, whether acid, alkaline, or neutral. To ensure early success, start with locally proven types and insert marginally hardy temptations sparingly. You should experiment, of course, since there are always exceptions to the rules, but only in small doses as you gain the practical knowledge all gardeners eventually obtain.

Before doing the actual planting, make a sketch of your intended arrangement to guide your placements as well as to figure out how many plants you will need for the size of the bed or border. Position selections for a border in descending order of mature heights, with the tallest in the rear (or in the center if the bed is free-standing), the lowest in front, and those of middling height residing in between. To gain greater visual bulk, group a minimum of three identical plants into triangular arrangements throughout the planting space. This allows for you to collect a bouquet now and then without disrupting the garden effect. At some point or another throughout the growing season, a portion of any perennial arrangement will be out of flower, and so the leafy aftermath must be evaluated, too, for its value as to shape, texture, and color interest. (This is where summer annuals can become real helpmeets.)

Although every hardiness zone has local plant preferences to draw upon, the following planting outline offers a list of widely adaptable perennials for noticeable flower display in a full-sun exposure for several months. Naturally, the dimensions of your planting area will influence how many of these perennials you can comfortably fit together, but at least you will gain some idea about which companionable choices can offer seasonal bands of bloom. Various color options usually exist within any main plant category for those of you seeking particular limits to your rainbow parade.

To begin, make a same-plant or mixed border line of these early spring, foreground perennials (later-blooming ones will just now be emerging): basket-of-gold (*Aurinia saxatilis*), rock cress (*Arabis*), or moss phlox (*Phlox subulata*), perhaps joined with some crocus, early tulips, or other small bulbs for further color and interest. Late spring blossoming can be provided by hardy carnation (*Dianthus*), sea pink (*Armeria*), and candytuft (*Iberis*).

The middle bed area can supply late spring to summer interest from the

The flower heads of 'Autumn Joy' sedum remain attractive for months into late autumn.

modestly sized peony (*Paeonia*), Shasta daisy (*Leucanthemum ×superbum*), various iris, and tall veronica. Midsummer accents of garden phlox (*Phlox paniculata*), bee balm (*Monarda*), and daylily (*Hemerocallis*) offer a wide assortment of colorful selections. The early autumn emphasis arrives with dwarf aster (*Aster* Oregon-Pacific Strain), autumn anemone (*Anemone ×hybrida*), hardy chrysanthemum (*Dendranthema*), and stonecrop (*Sedum*).

For the background (or center) area use delphinium, foxglove (*Digitalis*), coneflower (*Echinacea*), and heliopsis as summertime bloom, followed by the billowing mass of tall asters (*Aster novae-angliae*) and boltonia for autumnal showiness. Any delphinium in this mix may rebloom in the cooler days of autumn, and the garden phlox will set smaller side shoots of new flowers if kept deadheaded at all times. Of course, you can readily scatter clumps of summer bulbs throughout the bed to gain both showy flowering and fragrance from June into September. The lily group includes both the vivid but non-scented Asiatic hybrids (*Lilium* Mid-Century Hybrids) for late June and July and the heavily perfumed Oriental hybrids (*Lilium auratum* and *L. speciosum*) for August and early September, though their grand heights probably will require some staking.

Special accents can also be provided by various ornamental grasses, which produce many styles of airy and durable seed heads on long stems by late summer to mid-autumn. Attractive selections from this newly popular plant group include the foot-high blue fescue (*Festuca glauca*) and the slightly taller Japanese blood grass (*Imperata cylindrica*), along with the modest-sized feather reed grass (*Calamagrostis ×acutiflora*) and dwarf fountain grass (*Pennisetum*). The very tall and widely expansive Japanese silver grass (*Miscanthus*), as well as pampas grass (*Cortaderia*), probably belong elsewhere on the property.

Ferns are ground cover plants of special distinction and value. A goodly number of hardy ferns suitable either for full sun or dappled light offer yet another remarkable set of seed-head and leafy attractions. They range in height from several inches to 2 feet, are evergreen or deciduous, often show attractive autumn colors, and occasionally produce sturdy fruiting members useful for indoor decoration. Some prefer very damp sites, while others are quite content on a sun-baked hillside. Every garden has some spot where ferns, alone or in combination with other plants, can become a handsome addition. They may not flower, but they have fascinating foliage displays.

Midsummer Asiatic lilies vibrate with color but not scent.

The wide-spreading Japanese silver grass (*Miscanthus*) creates its attractive seed heads in mid-autumn.

A major drawback of these mostly seasonal plants, however, is their tendency to disappear from view by early winter in many areas. The effect of killing frost or built-in dormancy then produces large empty spaces in a garden. For out-of-view locations, such voids may be of little concern, but if the gaps are visible from main house windows for months on end, then you have a visual handicap requiring a more interesting resolution. A simple adjustment is to fill-in the emptiness with an occasional evergreen or deciduous modest-sized shrub to supply some twiggy shadow lines. Losing a little display space for flowers seems a small price to pay for gaining visual comfort.

The delicate foliage tracery of maidenhair fern (*Adiantum*) is fascinating as a shade accent.

Chapter 9

Selecting Plants for Gardens

Plant material of every type can cooperatively fit a multitude of our landscape needs because plants are not just highly attractive but also functional as problem solvers. Plants serve to anchor eroding slopes, diminish forceful winds, screen out unwanted views, contribute welcome shade, soften architectural bareness, seductively scent the air, produce stimulating splashes of seasonal color, and provide sturdy ground covers and cooling carpets for outdoor play or entertaining. Without these dependable and adaptable plants to aid us, we would certainly have a much more trying existence.

But with the bewildering array of different plants available for garden use, you may feel that choosing and arranging your plants correctly is an overwhelming task beyond your capacities. Rest assured, it need not be so daunting if you simplify your approach in an orderly fashion. We all have to begin somewhere.

The first task, of course, is to establish priorities about which of your special garden concerns require the quickest resolution from additional planting. Useful shade, privacy screening, windbreaks, and erosion control normally have more garden value than just increasing the decorative contribution—valuable as that is—but combining the practical and the aesthetic in your choices is the best approach. After all, a single shade tree can supply both sun relief and a bit of neighborly screening while also providing some striking autumn foliage color, especially when you seek out such bonuses from maple, birch, aspen, or cottonwood.

If providing year-round privacy is an important consideration in your garden development, you will need to rely on evergreen material, but if shading a portion of the house is the primary concern, then you have alternatives. A deciduous tree is faster growing and allows winter sunlight to penetrate the windows of your house and also warm the roof, while an evergreen tree requires more growth time but produces consistent shadowing. By summer either tree type will effectively cool your home and help reduce air-conditioning costs. Naturally, the plant's purchase size, its annual expansion rate, and the initial spacing influence how quickly you will gain the results you seek. For both privacy screening and shade relief in the shortest time, the best approach is to install the largest plants you can afford.

Once you determine priorities and set a workable budget, you then need to explore your choices in greater detail. Planting design involves living material, and so a keen understanding of all aspects related to horticultural care is a vital

Plants contribute shade, screening, seasonal color, and useful carpeting for gardens in every locale.

portion of garden knowledge. Since you obviously want your plants to thrive with a minimum of fuss, you have to learn which ones behave best in your hardiness zone, soil conditions, and rainfall levels as well as in your intended placement on the site. Observing plants already growing well in your neighborhood is a good place to begin, and with a little social interaction about these plants you will gain a surprising amount of additional knowledge about the pleasures and pitfalls of local gardening. All garden enthusiasts enjoy sharing their know-how. In addition, you should faithfully read books and periodicals about plant care, attend some plant-focused lectures, and make repeated excursions to your local arboretum or nursery display garden for further guidance about practical landscape choices. A lot of willingly shared information is out there for you to take in, so do not hesitate to utilize it freely. In truth, the only way you can ever really know enough about how to provide the finest conditions for your planting investment is through continual learning. The more you learn, the more you profit.

Of course you will want to avoid troublesome plants, and every geographic area has its share, so keep a list of all prior recommendations and evaluate each by inquiry and by reading about them in books and periodicals. For example, silver maple (*Acer saccharinum*) and poplar (*Populus*) can certainly provide shade or screening in a hurry, but each has brittle stems easily cracked or broken off by ice and wet snow. Boxelder (*Acer negundo*) and Siberian elm (*Ulmus pumila*) seem to rain down snapped twigs in quantity during every wind storm. Mulberry (*Morus*) and buckthorn (*Rhamnus*), along with some palms, drop squishy fruit through much of the summer and readily stain nearby walks, terraces, and driveways. Consistent disease attacks and insect pest infestations detract mightily from any plant's effectiveness, and a sickly or disfigured specimen is very difficult to hide. Identify what growth handicaps persist in your region, and shy away from using those plants that are too costly of your time, money, and enjoyment.

By this point you may recognize that the once-daunting list of potential plants can dwindle somewhat once you make serious evaluations about their true worth for your area. Nevertheless, your reduced roster will likely still retain enough attractive plants for you to make personal choices to suit your design ideas. Installing only the "best of the best" should be your goal, and some focused knowledge is all that is required to achieve that goal.

Types of Vegetation

The world is covered with three main types of vegetation: trees, shrubs, and ground covers. These exist in unequal distributions throughout the growing regions of the globe as both naturalized and created collections. The tree group, consisting of both evergreen and deciduous forms, includes the tallest representatives, with a gigantic California redwood (*Sequoia*) recently measured as topping out at 385 feet. In general, trees have a single, indivisible, woody trunk. Multistemmed trees are not overly common in Nature, and where seen in the wild may actually be the chance outcome of several identical seeds germinating tightly together to form a clump. Another explanation for such anomalies may involve a ground-level disease that stunted the main upward growth, forcing the side shoots to take over and make a cluster. Yet this multiplicity of stems also may be simply the remains from animal browsing when a seedling was young and juicy for eating. In any event, a tree usually maintains just one upright trunk, and many reach great heights.

While some plant authorities restrict a shrub to heights of 15 feet or less and then say that any further growth makes it a small tree, to me shrubs are best defined as woody plants that consistently produce multiple, somewhat equal-sized stems rising from the base at ground level—but with no definitive height limitation. Whatever its specific definition, a shrub, like a tree, usually cannot be divided down the middle to create additional plants. Exceptions do exist, of course, in shrubs that expand in such a way as to provide removable and plantable off-shoots. The wild shrub roses and common lilacs, for example, maintain extensive, spreading habits as a result of many roaming, underground stems called suckers, which can be sliced free from the parent without harm. This growth habit is rare among shrubs, however, and new plants ordinarily are commercially created from sowing seeds or from stem cuttings.

Ground covers are somewhat complicated to categorize accurately. After all, any spreading plant does cover some part of the ground. Nevertheless, ground covers are usually thought of as low, constantly expanding plants, both evergreen and deciduous, with a remarkable diversity that includes shrubs, vines, grasses, ferns, bulbs, herbaceous perennials, annuals, mosses, and yes, even the weeds. Mowable grass turf is the most common ground cover in gardens for its ease of growing and for its simple repair technique (either by reseeding or sodding), but its greater attribute is its suitability for walking on in any weather. When lawn maintenance becomes a true burden, however, many homeowners begin a search for preferable substitutions.

PRIMACY OF TREES AND SHRUBS

The prime focus of any garden design should be its trees and shrubs. Due to their greater height, width, and longevity, trees create the major emphasis in a setting while also serving such subsidiary purposes as providing shade and screening. However, since trees are slow to reach maturity and thus to present their full value, any new tree additions to a site should receive first priority in your planting program. You will benefit more quickly if you purchase the largest size your budget can manage. When placing trees, provide sufficient room for expansion so that both future roots and branching can form normal spreads, and always avoid crowding trees too close to buildings.

Treasure and preserve any aged tree specimen already on your property that is in good health and shape since its landscape contribution will not be matched

Here new trees are placed with respect for future root and branch expansion.

in your lifetime by any new planting. Respect its sturdy ability to reach this age, and your subsequent design additions should highlight the noteworthy qualities of the established tree specimens. Of course, not every existing old tree is worth retaining just because it has life and a noticeable presence. Disease, insect pests, air or soil pollution, and crowding from other plants can easily destroy or reduce the vigor of any salvaged tree. Consult with a reputable arborist early in your garden renovation if you have any doubts about a tree's future.

All trees or shrubs located near areas that will receive extensive work deserve more than casual regard if they are to survive in good shape. It can take years to restore damaged bark or to repair extensively cut roots. Earth modeling, both cut and fill operations, can have a major impact on plant health and often cause future difficulties (see also "Earth Grading" in Chapter 3). Any excessive soil removal within the branch spread of a tree exposes the delicate feeder roots to additional unexpected air and sunlight. Cutting away the prime support roots in construction activity will also seriously weaken the ability of woody plants to withstand future storms successfully. Similarly, deep earth fill around a tree or shrub can interrupt the plant's normal breathing mechanisms and cause slow suffocation. This additional soil mass contributes an extra burden of weight on close-to-the-surface roots that are intimately involved in the regular oxygen and moisture exchanges necessary for continued good growth. Any plant will struggle to survive after harsh treatment, but half-alive items surely are not on your agenda. Correct techniques for handling necessary site adjustments are available, so investigate and plan with care to minimize damage to each salvaged tree or shrub. All the parts of a plant exist for a reason according to the code of Nature, and they should not be ignored in any garden renovation.

Trees or major shrubs that you wish to retain occasionally end up either too low or too high at their original grades compared to any adjacent new grading work. Often the best solution is to transplant the material to a more suitable location, but if this is impractical, then an alternative is to construct retaining walls of masonry or heavy timber around the plants. To hold back an embankment of new grading near a lower-elevation tree, construct a semicircular barrier wall as far as possible from the trunk. Having a full-circle tree well would trap too much rain, ice, or snow and would prove detrimental to the tree within a short time. A tree or shrub remaining appreciably raised above the revised grading needs similar assistance from a wall to prevent excessive soil erosion and the drying out of the feeder roots. Again, to allow for continued root expansion, provide a generous soil area by locating this retaining wall as far as possible from the base of the plant, preferably out to the drip line of the branches. Special watering attention may also be needed to aid the plants toward speedy recovery. No one enjoys watching a plant endure a slow death, but unless you are fully aware of the effects of major grading efforts, you could start the process. A proper design approach includes genuine concern for all the ingredients of your garden program.

LAWN AND DECORATIVE GROUND COVERS

No planned development provides greater breadth and dignity to a garden setting than a stretch of well-kept grass turf, and nothing is more restful to the eye than a cool greensward. Lawn should always be seen from major viewing areas of the house since it conveys an impression of welcoming outdoor space for both active use and visual enjoyment. Where it can be grown successfully without an inordinate amount of fuss, excess watering, and maintenance cost, grass lawn is a highly appropriate and well-enjoyed carpet for a garden setting.

Unifying various parts of a garden design in an eye-comforting way, a neatly mowed lawn consistently invites you to walk across it toward other garden interests. When laid in generous sheets, its smooth perfection can knit together the many usual bed outlines of the ground layout in a remarkably simple way. Its uniform coloring and consistent texture provides a bland but useful contrast to the various silhouettes, foliage and flower shapes, or colorations from nearby architectural or planting accents. We also thoroughly enjoy romping, strolling, and entertaining on its cool, cushiony surface. Lawns of uniform quality can perform minor miracles of landscape improvement, besides eliminating dust and mud from the scene.

However, since a sizable lawn area is composed of thousands of similar plants jammed together in a one-crop demand for attention, along with requiring consistently heavy and costly watering to maintain it, lawn care is without doubt a time-consuming and repetitive-need activity, whether you perform the chores yourself or pay for outside maintenance help. Reducing your garden work load is always a logical move when plant upkeep becomes too tiresome or too expensive to be enjoyable, and using substitute planting or even paving for parts of the existing lawn might become part of your garden evaluation.

Any troublesome-to-tend lawn areas—steep slopes, increasingly shady spots, or consistently worn and compacted trails—can be readily converted to other types of ground cover, whether evergreen or deciduous and shrubby or vinelike. Such a shift in plant material can introduce not only alternative textures and colors but perhaps some useful flower interest. A wide range of creeping junipers, low-spreading cotoneasters, viney euonymus, ferns, and heathers are commonly available and offer durable and highly decorative lawn substitutes. On the acre lot of my current home I have reduced the original lawn area to half its size in twenty years by turning over some of the grassy openness into more interesting seasonal beds of textural and flowering interest, in both full sun and semishade, at no loss to the overall design.

In areas where growing a reliable lawn becomes either impractical or ridiculously costly to establish and maintain, and where other ground covers do not allow for convenient walking on, you may want to install wide, paved walkways of weather-durable materials such as stone, brick, concrete, or tile. Even

Extensive heather (*Erica*) planting offers color, texture, and lower maintenance than grass lawn.

loose pebbles laid on a firmly packed sand or stone dust base is a useful alternative, as is several inches of a loose, organic material such as pine bark placed on smoothly raked soil, which is no more than creating an unplanted garden bed. Thick turf is superior for many garden designs, but for areas where it would not be practical, seek out one of several harmonious alternatives.

Plant Outlines and Garden Meanings

Identifying the general outline or silhouette of a plant is a useful place to start learning about plant types before evaluating their finer details. Of greater importance is recognizing the value of the plant for your own garden intentions, since the shape or mass of a plant is a major building block for every landscape picture. Which silhouette or bulk you select, as well as where you place it, greatly influences how much you have actually improved your garden setting. Some choices will be strongly assertive while others will prove timid in their effects. Each plant selection needs to be balanced or contrasted properly with its neighbors at all times in form, size, texture, or color value. It is vital that you carefully study the inherent natural qualities in every plant shape before you actually combine them. Your resulting design should carry your eye back and forth across the layout harmoniously. Each of the many shapes in a landscape puzzle has to blend not only with other plants but with any adjacent architectural element as well, and some of these existing elements are not easily changed.

Tall plant outlines offered by pines, spruces, or columnar shade trees will direct your eye upward, while horizontal forms, particularly hedges, direct your vision across an area. Those plants with full-foliaged, well-defined shapes often benefit visually from close proximity to looser, billowing outlines, and deliberately combining them establishes effective contrasts. With formal details such as clipped hedges and sheared topiary pieces, the plant forms may also assume crisp architectural expressions, which can reinforce a garden design concept. Informal compositions often utilize a greater number of natural plant silhouettes to capture your interest. The opportunity to include many different plant forms in a design can prove rewarding when the elements are harmoniously blended, and not used to excess. Freedom of expression is not a license for overkill. Each successful garden design must establish boundaries of proper visual proportions.

Keep in mind that while evergreen shapes provide year-round importance with their leafy fullness, deciduous ones may diminish in landscape value when their leaves drop. Although the summer foliage undoubtedly reinforces a deciduous plant's appeal by adding texture and color to the outline, a mass of barren stems and twigs throughout the dormant season may prove less fascinating. Of course, the arrangement and color value of such empty branches could reveal new attractions, especially from mature shade trees or specimen shrubs such as canoe birch (*Betula papyrifera*) or crape myrtle (*Lagerstroemia*), both of which have noteworthy bark. In any case, you should be aware of these seasonal adjustments and provide prominently viewed locations with a maximum of appealing winter silhouettes.

Both natural and hybridized plants fit into a number of common categories of outlines or silhouettes, each of which adds different dimensions to a garden setting. These include columnar to fastigiate (Lombardy poplar, *Populus nigra* 'Italica'), conical to pyramidal (Bradford pear, *Pyrus calleryana* 'Bradford'), round to oval (Norway maple, *Acer platanoides*), vase-shaped to inverted pyra-

Deciduous plants create columnar, dome-shaped, and open-headed silhouettes.

A weeping cherry (*Prunus subhirtella* 'Pendula') specimen gracefully displaying its early spring flowers.

Prostrate and fountainlike junipers grow cooperatively in the modest shade beneath scattered trees.

mid (Kousa dogwood, *Cornus kousa*), pendulous to weeping (weeping willow, *Salix alba* var. *vitellina*), dense to open-headed (European beech, *Fagus sylvatica*), irregular to distorted (Japanese red pine, *Pinus densiflora*), outward ascending to fountainlike (Van Houtte spirea, *Spiraea* ×*vanhouttei*), and prostrate to flattened (blue rug juniper, *Juniperus horizontalis* 'Blue Rug').

Tree and shrub outlines additionally contribute a sense of garden meaning or mood association by their outward appearances. These include such evaluations as rugged or delicate, flamboyant or somber, and wistful or elegant, depending entirely upon the personality of the observer, the season of the year, the current weather conditions, plus any other complexity of personal interest or timing. Mood response, obviously, has many interpretations and varies widely.

Hedges

A hedge is a centuries-old, barrier planting idea of totally human invention, simply composed of identical woody plant material tightly spaced. Whether lofty or low in height and whether regularly trimmed or left natural, a hedge is rightly called a "living fence" or a "wall of greenery." Since density and continuity are the primary requirements of a hedge, the potential individual silhouette or specimen is surrendered by this deliberate crowding to create a solid, uniform ribbon. Originally conceived as an easy-to-concoct defense against human intrusion or else to pen livestock conveniently and economically with local plant material, such hedges, or hedgerows, cleverly featured impressive thorniness. Bushy hawthorn trees (*Crataegus*) were a common favorite throughout early European history, with their intertangled branching and long, needle-like spines.

Nowadays most hedge installations are far less threatening in their appearance and are planted in gardens mainly as attractive visual obstructions to provide privacy, restrict casual trespassing, or emphasize the enclosure details of a formal design. While many hedges are placed primarily to mark a boundary, any sizable length and height of hedging can also contribute an architectural frame or a backdrop for important landscape features such as statuary or a fountain. A hedge can agreeably provide seasonal flowering or winter fruiting and perhaps autumn foliage color as well. It is worth investigating how you can gain several features from a plant selection at no additional cost.

Columnar arborvitae (*Thuja*) arranged as an unclipped hedge.

Tightly sheared yew (*Taxus*) makes a true "wall of greenery."

When it comes time for the actual hedge planting, you do well to prepare a continuous trench, not individual plant pits, with an equal depth of organically enhanced soil, to provide quicker and more even growth. Plants ordered from the nursery inevitably will exhibit some variability of both height and spread, and the prepared trench allows for easier on-site adjustments. The ideal spacing depends upon the intended need for the hedge (whether a simple barrier or a privacy screen), the type of plant chosen, and certainly the initial purchase size. An often-used rule of spacing is to have the individual plants just touching if you need an immediate effect, but you might do better to take into account the typical annual growth rate along with the expected mature size of the selection in your locale. Since the feeder roots of evergreens are concentrated near the top

Formal garden designs often benefit from neat hedge enclosures, such as this *Taxus ×media* 'Hatfieldii' hedge.

of the soil, for example, crowding many plants together will create excess competition for moisture and nutrients and may produce a noticeable loss of bottom branching after a decade or so. More generous spacing at the beginning, even if it means a less solid hedge, can produce longer-lasting satisfaction.

Slowly expanding trees and dwarf shrubs, whether evergreen or deciduous, can be planted close together, but rapid-growing deciduous trees or shrubs should be set farther apart at installation since they have greater annual growth. Just about any tree or shrub can be trained into a satisfactory hedge given patience and regular care, and so you must always select material with clearly understood growth characteristics to ensure that any after-care needs fit your budgeted time, energy, and money. Plants with exuberant natures will continue to show that wild abandon into the future, just as those with messy fruit drop will continue to be nuisances year after year. Plants with prickly or even dangerously sharp thorns need special evaluation beforehand if placed next to public walkways, private drives, or on property lines. These threatening characteristics apply whether the plant is used for hedging or set individually—hedges are just more of one kind together—so choose and locate your hedging plants wisely.

Hedges placed within the root zone of large trees often show a marked reduction of uniform growth within a short time. As expected, a mass of established tree roots collects most of the available soil water and nutrients within its growing range, and introducing a long line of hedge plants to this area will handicap the introduced hedge but not the tree. The tree also provides some shading of the hedge for several hours each day. Digging into the tree's major roots for the hedge installation can do more harm than good for both plants, and under these cramped conditions you would do better to erect a fence.

When shaping a hedge into a formally pruned line, you should take into account that adequate sunlight must consistently reach the oldest and lowest branches if they are to remain dense and effectively attractive. You can accomplish this simply by tapering the outside portions to provide a slightly wider bottom than top. Any initial hedge shearing should be postponed until the plants have had a full growing season to adjust to their new location and then should be started only when the following year's growth has extended 6 inches, depending upon the plant. Such pruning involves halting the terminal or upward growth in order to stimulate the axillary or side buds to expand and create fuller density. Thereafter the trimming schedule should be determined by the local growth rate, the amount of desired neatness, and the labor costs.

In some mild climates four prunings a year is considered normal, but most hedges in other areas usually need only two to remain attractive. The first pruning is often made in early spring to restore any parts damaged by winter's rigors, while the second is normally set to control growth by mid-autumn. With spring- and early summer-blossoming deciduous or broadleaf evergreen material, schedule pruning for just after flowering is completed. Any late-season shaping here will remove the following season's blossom buds, so limit this pruning to just simple neatness.

Established hedges of unwanted size present some puzzling problems about how to reduce them without harming future growth. Aged evergreens rarely take kindly to severe pruning since the remaining older stem wood will not always resprout new growth in regular fashion. In addition, because the inner bark of older evergreens had been shaded by its foliage cover, the abrupt removal of this former sun and wind shield can dehydrate these stems. Complete rejuvenation in a short time may prove impossible, or at least erratic, and you could be better off ripping out the old and bringing in a new hedge altogether. With deciduous material, drastic pruning for renewal is often workable, depending, as always, on the type of plant involved, since these plant types tend to replenish lost stems and growth buds far more easily than evergreens. Yet here, too, overaged plants may not be worth such rejuvenation effort given the somewhat unclear results, and replanting with younger stock could be the wiser option.

Espaliers

By selective and patient pruning over a modest period of time, both evergreen and deciduous trees or tall shrubs can be trained to grow attractively flat in one plane against a support wall or trellis in a form known as an espalier. Originating centuries ago in ancient Rome with fruit trees deliberately shaped to conserve ground space as well as to increase crop yield, such highly ornamental pieces are not only fascinating to see but often produce the bonus of faster-ripening fruit, aided by the heat-retentive backdrops. Once the pruning outline

Candelabra pruning for a wall-attached fruiting apple (*Malus*).

is established, they require only annual trimming attention, but that service must be maintained on a regular basis or else the plant will quickly revert to its original, natural shape, often within just a year.

For espaliers, use plants that already have narrow and normally upright branching or at least maintain a large quantity of side shoots. Choose a wall-mounting space that offers sufficient room for reasonable expansion over the years on a site with appropriate sunlight for the selected plant, and then anchor the plant to its support securely. Use soft ties around the stems, leaving some extra room for normal stem expansion. You can also install espaliers on wire supports strung through a sturdy wood or metal frame, creating a single, free-standing attraction or even combining them into a continuous fence, perhaps to mask a work area or as a novel backdrop in a vegetable patch. Wherever you position this useful conversation piece, treat it intelligently as a solution to a garden need that harmonizes with the rest of its setting. Overuse of this pruning technique can be intrusive.

An espaliered yew (*Taxus*) is a highly decorative evergreen feature.

Plants in Containers

Where ground-level planting space is inadequate for your design needs, container planting makes a valid substitution with wide appeal. Various pots, tubs, and boxes can be used as decorative aboveground holders of plant roots, but the living material within becomes largely dependent on human care for survival. No containerized plant flourishes as vigorously or as long as one in open ground—except, possibly, the short-season annuals—yet potted material does attractively resolve many garden design problems, especially if the style and quality of the container also contributes some value to the scene.

Container soil not only ages poorly over time but also dries out much more

A crabapple (*Malus*) tree, a dwarf rhododendron, and creeping juniper combine effectively in this large planter.

quickly from wind action on the exposed sides of the pot or box. Constantly expanding roots will eventually fill even the largest container, particularly those roots from small trees and vigorous shrubs, and they also exhaust the nutrient value of the soil in a relatively short time. When dense root mats fill the available soil space, providing adequate moisture for continued growth becomes difficult. At such times the irrigation water tends to flow down the wall of the container, only grazing the root ball, and drains quickly out through the bottom drainage holes. Once in this strained growing condition, a potted plant may partially defoliate or at least show restricted growth. The solution is to transplant the material to a larger container at least 6 inches wider and deeper, depending upon the particular type and vigor of the plant involved, or else to transfer some or all of the tubbed collection to a garden location and begin again in the container with younger or less-active selections. Just keep in mind that any potted plant will eventually outgrow its container size.

One consideration not always made clear in catalogs and garden centers is the durability of the container material itself. Clay pots, whether glazed or not, often crack or disintegrate from prolonged exposure to winter cold. Composite materials are generally more weather-tolerant, but they are inconsistent, too, if the temperature drops well below freezing, becoming trial-and-error experiments. There is a difference between "weather resistant" and "weatherproof," but this distinction may have to be learned through experience. Wood, resin plastic, and stone, however, are reliable container materials unfazed by weather extremes and can be safely left outdoors year-round in almost every area.

Plant Positioning

Along with selecting the most adaptable plants, you need to value the significance of correct positioning of your material. Both distance and perspective alter some desirable plant features as you look about a garden. The fine-needled hemlock, as an example, loses its textural distinction when set far away from view, becoming a solid, but feathery, outline. Any item set close by reveals its details for greater appreciation, so determine beforehand which feature, its mass or its detail, is more important to emphasize.

Leaf size is another design factor involved here. Whether evergreen or deciduous, those plants carrying large-sized and conspicuous volumes of foliage, such as Catawba rhododendron (*Rhododendron catawbiense*) or horse chestnut (*Aesculus*), will noticeably project themselves toward you, but plants with finer, smaller leaves, such as honeylocust (*Gleditsia*) and most evergreen azaleas, tend to recede. In a confined garden space, fine textures in the foreground establish a sense of greater visual distance because the eye travels over them quickly toward points of bolder interest, especially to those plants with seasonal color features. When you place large-leaved material close to a main viewing point, you create the illusion of reduced foreground space. With this nugget about depth perception, you can visually enlarge or diminish landscape distances by foliage sizes, just as you can with juxtaposing colors (see Chapter 6). It is a simple but effective garden design tool.

Fine-textured plants in the foreground of a view suggest greater visual distance.

Producing greater spaciousness for a limited land area can also be accomplished by correct plant positioning. Since your eyes move across spatial emptiness such as open lawn until stopped by some object or distraction, you do well to avoid negating that space with interruptions, no matter how attractive their special characteristics may be. Instead, place your prime selections on the sidelines to frame your open view.

As discussed earlier, proper plant positioning requires careful evaluation of the expected future expansion of the material and whether it will later interfere with the full use of work or play spaces as well as walks and terraces. Consider, too, whether your daily activities might hamper or damage the plants as they enlarge, since compacted soil, volumes of piled snow, and generally abused stems and foliage can disrupt the plant's expected show of attractiveness. The practical aspects of positioning have just as much validity in a garden as the aesthetic ones.

Seasonal Assets

Every growing area offers a wealth of plants to bloom at staggered times, and so you can readily arrange these display sequences for your own purposes to supply even the most modest garden area with on-going interest and appeal throughout the seasons. If there is insufficient space for a grand collection of floriferous woody plants sequentially in bloom (or fruit), incorporate other showy but smaller-sized substitutes. Spring and summer bulbs, herbaceous perennials, annuals, ferns, and ornamental grasses supply similar blossom and textural stimulations, and of course these items should also be intermixed in gardens that do allow many woody shrubs.

Nevertheless, impressive flowering is only one of the appeals delivered by plants. Those with more than one season of attractive features, such as showy fruit crops or glowing leaf color, increase your garden pleasure. For example, the striking, orange-to-gold, autumn foliage of witchhazel (*Hamamelis*) is just as prominent as its late-winter-into-spring mass of showy blooms lining the many sturdy stems. The durable brightness of the heavy clusters of pyracantha fruit, lasting well into winter dormancy, reasonably matches the plant's generous bursts of creamy spring flowers. An appealing glow of rich red or deep yellow from the barren stems of either Siberian or goldentwig shrub dogwoods

(*Cornus alba* and *C. stolonifera* 'Flaviramea') contribute a wintertime bonus that actually exceeds the value of their summertime flowering. The deep rose-colored 'Autumn Joy' sedum is also a dual-season contributor with its stiffly held stems supporting mahogany pancakes of seedheads for months.

Such extra-season benefits belong in your garden planning, especially where winter dormancy is prolonged. We all need a series of perky garden pleasures as we patiently await the return of new growth, and the potential from dual-season plants can help our spirits survive in much better shape. It pays to seek them out.

Effects of Shade

Shade is inevitably part of every garden and landscape scene, whether it arrives as shadows from buildings, large trees and shrubs, or walls and fences. By its degree of intensity, shade can be divided into *full, deep, half,* and *light.* Full shade

Deep shade is troublesome but not unworkable for gaining some flowering response.

is year-round dimness at ground level from the dominating light-obstruction produced mainly by solid structures and all sorts of tall, dense evergreens climbing toward maturity. Here the soil will remain cooler and damper far longer into the growing season.

Deep shading usually arrives with the dense summertime foliage of many deciduous trees or wide-spreading, tall shrubs, plus an occasional evergreen tree, but here some increased light intensity does manage to penetrate regularly to the ground from late autumn until mid-spring, when the majority of such plants are leafless. Half shade is a reasonably equalized proportion of full sun and deep shade. It is workable for a wide variety of plant material, but you need to determine the duration of the bright light on the area during summertime growth. You will receive much more productive plant performance if the sun's

Half shade at noon creates important differences in light intensity.

heat and brightness appear in the late-morning and mid-afternoon hours. Light shading, the easiest type of all to handle, is simply open sunlight filtered for brief periods by deciduous plants with either sparse crowns or delicate foliage.

Needle evergreens rarely thrive in full shade but rather grow increasingly sparse and leggy as they seek out more sunlight. Broadleaf kinds do better in shade, particularly the ground cover sorts. If you have deep shading, however, the list of plantable needle evergreens improves, including these reasonably adaptable examples: Japanese yew (*Taxus cuspidata*), Harrington plum yew (*Cephelotaxus harringtonia*), Canada hemlock (*Tsuga canadensis*), and Mission arborvitae (*Thuja occidentalis* 'Techny'), and each will adjust surprisingly well to full sun. Broadleaf evergreens that perform happily in deep shade include the majority of the rhododendron clan, Japanese holly (*Ilex crenata*), camellia, aucuba, and mountain laurel (*Kalmia*). Ground cover evergreens workable in this greatly reduced light embrace many well-used favorites such as English ivy (*Hedera helix*), pachysandra, myrtle (*Vinca*), creeping lilyturf (*Liriope*), and Christmas fern (*Polystichum acrostichoides*). The most widely planted herbaceous perennial for all types of shade is the plantain lily (*Hosta*), which offers a truly generous spread of foliage enhancements along with mid- to late-summer flowering spikes.

Half shade favorably suits an enormous number of plant types, and examples are readily locatable in almost every nursery or plant catalog. Naturally, all the plants tolerant of deep shade also appreciate any upgrading in light intensity and probably will reward you with greater flowering and stronger growth. By the same token, as a site's half shade edges closer to deep shading with the vigorous expansion of nearby trees and tall shrubs, the half-shade-tolerant plants may struggle. The increasing light reduction can produce diminished flower production, thinner foliage, and leggier silhouettes. The amount of shade is obviously a variable and not a constant factor.

You can, however, improve some light encroachments by careful pruning. Thinning the crown of dense-foliaged, deciduous trees—without compromising their silhouette value by excessive removal of branches—is a common practice, but there is less possibility of an attractive end result with shapely needle or broadleaf evergreens, which are the biggest shade-producing offenders. Drastic pruning of these plants will create noticeable losses in their natural silhouette and character, becoming oddities no one needs in any garden. Unless you are willing to cut down such dominant evergreens for more light, you should tolerate the situation as part of the natural order and make adjustments.

Soil Moisture Adaptation

Soil moisture is essential for all plants, as you know, but if some of your property is consistently soggy most of the year you have an important horticultural problem to resolve. Normally if the situation is minor, you can improve conditions by raising the grade with additional soil, but underground drainage lines may be required if the area of wetness is sizable and obvious. Of course, you also have to find a place to transfer this water to within your property, and if this is unworkable, then you will have to limit your plant selections here to those tolerant of "wet feet." Unfortunately, this does not offer a very large collection of options.

Any plants already growing thriftily within these special moisture conditions, and that have landscape value for your design plans, should be left as found and worked into the development. Establishing new plant material into such oxygen-deprived and constantly damp soil is usually a troublesome endeavor. Keep in mind, too, that any nursery-grown selections, despite a known adaptability to "wet feet," will probably not have been raised on wet sites and will take time to adjust on your land. At least they will not need additional watering during dry spells.

Consistent dryness on a site, however, presents similar growing handicaps. The continually expanding roots of large trees and shrubs, a very sandy soil, and a consistently windy site all contribute to a drying-out of the conditions. You can remedy some of these factors with an annual top-dressing of decayed plant compost spread several inches deep over the entire dry area. When a volume of compost is not readily available, substitute a thick layer of other organic mulch material such as shredded bark, peanut hulls, or bagasse. Avoid spreading granular peat moss since it tends to crust easily and thus prevents rain from penetrating to the soil. Instead, dig peat into the soil to utilize its moisture-holding abilities.

Be aware that any plant introduced within the massed roots of existing material certainly needs to be adaptable and drought-tolerant to survive, especially through the first season. Each addition here will require generous and consistent irrigation until established, and this extra moisture, of course, will also encourage your existing plants to expand their roots even more. Whenever a plant dominates it does so at some cost to others nearby, regardless of the condition or location of the garden.

Shy away from planting shallow-rooted broadleaf evergreens on dry, rocky, or windswept sites since they expect much better growing conditions and will surely languish. Most of the needle evergreens respond far more cooperatively to these trying situations, especially the undaunted junipers. Reliably dependable for just about every geographic area of the United States and lower Canada in some form and selection, the evergreen junipers show amazing versatility and carry wide garden appeal whether a tree, shrub, or ground cover. The majority accept either dry or consistently damp locations, scorching or frosty wind blasts, full sun or moderate shading (the Chinese-origin sorts are the most cooperative in reduced light), and just about any soil type from acid to alkaline. Not surprisingly, juniper collections are found in nurseries everywhere in a wide variety of sizes, silhouettes, textures, and colorings. Many popular forms also produce showy and durable fruit crops annually. Junipers deserve your interest, especially if you want low upkeep.

Xeriscapes

With today's recurring drought scares and drinking-water shortages, along with the accompanying community watering restrictions, xeric or dry-gardening techniques are becoming increasingly viable and sensible approaches to garden design. Xeriscapes begin with all sorts of native plants that show ready adaptability to the amount of moisture provided only by natural rainfall. The list of plants suitable to dry landscapes in any region further encompasses nativelike types from other areas that have similar climates and soils.

While the xeriscape focus may at first seem more useful for semidesert or desert conditions, its practical application to other areas has much value. When you do not need to provide extra summertime irrigation for your plants' proper growth, you automatically reduce your maintenance costs, whether of time or money, and that is sensible conservation.

Attractive, drought-tolerant plants, from trees to ground covers, are widely promoted in nursery catalogs for intelligent and appealing incorporation into gardens. Granted, the flowers of native species may not be quite as large or as prolific as those of nursery-originated selections, but for blending a landscape into its natural habitat, native material is unsurpassed. Using xeric planting involves environmental awareness that brings its own satisfactions.

Overgrowth

One of the most common dilemmas in gardening that we all face at one time or another is unanticipated overgrowth. Each of us has at some point grossly underestimated the ultimate dimensions of a plant, which subsequently billows beyond its design need. To be sure, such strong growth indicates that the plants are content with both their placement and care and perhaps deserve some applause for their exuberance. Yet their continued presence in an out-of-scale state certainly challenges your design intent and requires some firm resolution. Invariably, foundation plantings (see also Chapter 10) are the worst offenders, with far too many examples to ignore.

Dry or xeric gardening is a sensible and attractive technique in many areas.

Excessive overgrowth may be the result of early impatience to have the land-scape and house quickly blend into the rest of the neighborhood scene, leading to improper spacing, or else it may be the result of the poorly planned inclusion of too many large, rapid-stretching choices—or possibly both. In any case, when you are unable to enjoy fully the architectural assets of your house—or even see out the windows—then your plantings are definitely overgrown. Now you require important revisions to restore order (see page 121).

Such a program might involve either the chore of constant pruning, which is unlikely to be practical or attractive with old plant material, or else reluctantly agreeing to the full removal (possibly with some exceptions) and replanting of this important garden area. Such an expensive learning experience points out once more that you should "know it before you grow it." Planting advice useful for every garden designer does not come any simpler than that.

Chapter 10

Foundation Planting

The now-common practice of adding a varied collection of plants around the exterior walls of a house, known as foundation planting, is a fairly recent innovation. As you may recall from Chapter 1, all shrubbery outlining a building was declared aesthetically unneeded during the eighteenth century in Great Britain, and that design proclamation was also faithfully followed in the colonial United States and Canada as well. The early-nineteenth-century American designer Alexander Jackson Downing also eliminated it from both his garden layouts and his writings as unnecessary site clutter. The general public, however, started dressing-up the exposed foundations of its sizable homes in a grander way only after the Victorian exuberance for planting all parts of a site became the fashion. We continue this approach today with equally good and ill results.

Several worthwhile aims can be attractively achieved by adding such foundation planting. The main objective is to blend the upright building comfortably with the relatively horizontal surrounding area and to knit the structure attractively to the ground. Planting additions do this very effectively, creating a logical harmony between these two important site elements by softening the boxy lines of the house, by accenting special features of the architectural style, and naturally, by beautifying the residential landscape. Remember, since no two houses and no two properties are identical, no two landscape treatments will be exactly alike either.

Before rushing out to buy any material for the foundation planting, however, you need to spend sufficient time carefully reviewing how well—or not—

your house and its site currently relate to one another. You may think of your intended planting scheme as the icing on the cake, but the cake has to be well made before the whole effect can be deemed successful. It is possible that you could benefit further, for example, by adjusting some awkward grading or by adding support walls to embankments before installing new trees and shrubbery. The main gist of this site review is to make certain that you have provided a physically and visually adequate foreground and platform around the building for your intended social and personal desires. If you have not fully clarified these needs, then now is the most economical time to do so, not later when plantings are already in place.

A one-story dwelling set on flat ground or gently rolling countryside is naturally reasonably well related to its land form, but a two-story house needs greater planning effort to wed it to the site because its vertical mass is far more evident. Of course, support planting is easier to arrange on flattish pieces of property, but houselots usually do not arrive so conveniently graded. For one, site irregularities such as steep frontage slopes or rocky outcrops and wooded patches need more than just some foundation planting to convincingly resolve the immediate problems of the drive approach and entry platform. The land around your house should be organized to do all it can for your planting concerns, your play and entertainment concerns, your parking concerns, and of course, your budget concerns. Only when all these logical site involvements are satisfied should you move toward "icing the cake." If complicated site adjustments are beyond your capacities or available time frame, then hire a professional for guidance. We all can use help from time to time in our garden design needs.

Because the front entry of a building is normally its most public face, your planting composition there should not only express your design skill but also the welcoming attitude of your own personality. The main walkway should be noticeable and safely walkable in all kinds of weather and should have sufficient night lighting (see also Chapter 3). Avoid incorporating plants with thorny stems or prickly foliage close to the walk, for obvious reasons. Space spreading plant material back far enough from this travelway so that no guest has to brush against wet, icy, or dusty foliage. In cold areas, allow some open space for the inevitable snow pile from clearing the walk.

If the entry area of your lot is favored with an attractive, large tree specimen,

Foundation planting here incorporates only occasional tall shrubs underplanted with evergreen azaleas in copious pachysandra and myrtle beds.

This sizable canoe birch (*Betula papyrifera*) supplies both scale and color value for planning the rest of the area.

utilize it to establish the scale and design direction for the other plant silhouettes, textures, and colorings contributing to this major element and to the
building. The solid anchoring presented by stone and brick houses seems even
more substantial when you include generous numbers of both needle and
broadleaf evergreens along the foundation, while wood-frame houses generally
benefit from a greater percentage of deciduous plants interwoven with appropriate evergreen selections. This design practice is probably the outcome of the
range of different colorings used on wood buildings, which are complemented
by the even wider selection of flower colors of deciduous material, but it also
suggests that a wood-framed structure looks more attractive when it does not
rise out of too many obscuring evergreens.

Unfortunately, a common practice on too many houselots is to line up new
foundation plants in a strict single file parallel to the building walls. Not only
does this often look awkward and stiff, but it also presents a layout that may
prove intrinsically weak, sparse, and often out of scale with the structure and its
site. It will hardly improve with age. The improper placement of an approach
walk too close to a home can contribute to the sparseness, and failing to recognize the proportions of open space needed for a proper foundation planting is
expensive to modify for a more generous spatial allotment. Such situations are
too often tolerated when they should be redesigned.

A far more suitable approach is to enlarge these frontage beds to hold at
least two rows or groupings of different-sized shrubs—and even three lines are
not out of place for sizable houses—with the tallest plants placed nearest to the
building to create a stepped-down arrangement toward the walk. To visually
anchor and soften the strong vertical lines at outer house corners, include a
small flowering tree or chunky evergreen specimen. Curiously, unless planted in
clusters, very narrowly upright needle evergreens do not contribute this same
corner-binding effect when used alone.

Foundation plants at any portion of the house should frame the windows,
not make them invisible over time. Give high value to your daily outlook from
inside the building and provide pleasant glimpses of your garden development
and enticing distant views, not the leggy backsides of vigorous shrubs. Do not
convince yourself that you can always trim back offending growth later, but instead pick out plants that will stay in proportion for your needs, and install them
where they will do the most good near your windows. Creating an ungraceful

The outlook from your windows should reveal attractive views, not woody plant stems.

Transplanting unneeded or overgrown foundation material can resolve other site needs.

collection of green "chicken croquettes" by constant shearing for growth control is a waste of time, effort, and plant material when more logical alternatives are readily available.

There will come a time on any established property, however, when the foundation shrubs and trees installed decades earlier may appear either too oversized or dowdy to keep in place any longer. Granted, bringing in a chain saw and backhoe for wholesale removals takes courage, but it provides a valid and sometimes valuable opportunity to orchestrate a new and more useful design scheme. Some of these seemingly overgrown plants nevertheless may have value to the site in other areas and should be relocated. While this transplanting operation may at first appear costly, you gain the worthwhile bonus of utilizing good-sized, functional specimens at far less expenditure than would come with buying a similar item at a nursery and having it installed. Furthermore, the existing plants are already well-adapted to your site, while a new group will require additional time to become adjusted. Do not overlook transfer possibilities in your renovation program. They can be highly productive and, perhaps, surprisingly affordable. After all, uniting the practical aspects with the aesthetic ones is what garden design is about.

Chapter 11

Five Years to Fulfillment: A Renovation Odyssey

Initially uninspiring, almost bald, and nearly flat, the rear portion of my third-acre, second-time-around houselot in suburban Boston, Massachusetts, eventually became a high-appeal oasis after five years of my hands-on effort and determination. Because the majority of the work for new grading, construction, and planting was done personally in spare time from my busy work and travel schedules as a landscape architect, the project took longer than I had originally anticipated. Too, the pinch of inadequate funding for it from time to time, along with the common disruptions from messy New England weather, added to the length of the time frame.

Similar problems surely exist for all homeowners with a do-it-yourself program. Endurance pays off, however, when you establish a reachable goal, have a well-developed plan of action, and accept a willingness to experiment and adjust to many changing circumstances. To create something worthwhile from nothing, you need a stout bundle of sincere motivation, sustained patience, and consistent enthusiasm. If any of these preliminary urges is lacking, you will be handicapped in achieving your dream garden.

My main concept here was to provide as much private, usable space for as many garden pleasures as possible while offering visual stimulation in all seasons. Rufus, my two-year-old German shepherd, had an inquisitive, wandering trait not entirely suited to my new neighbors' social interests, and so I had to make an early expenditure of some cost for a 6-foot, cedar stockade fence along the westerly property line, erected by a local supplier. The balance of this back

The flat, empty space at the start of the project.

The dog-restrictive cedar fence erected on the western property line.

lot was sealed by a wide-mesh wire fence attached to black-painted channel irons, which threaded through the background woodlot trees and attached to the side of the garage. This practically invisible wire fencing easily melted from sight and allowed some extended views into other abutters' land, making my lot appear larger. Besides, I did not want to be fully enclosed by solid fencing, wandering dog or not. Some planting of sizable needle evergreens quickly followed to screen the unaged wood fence.

Due to the natural stoniness of the skimpy existing soil in this area, along with the sluggish surface drainage from the flatness of the land, I decided to create modest mounds of fresh earth at the northerly end of the property for much of the intended new planting. This treatment avoided the puddling of rain water across the space and helped encourage faster root growth. As much as possible I tried to direct the water eastward into the adjoining woodlot. It was at this point that I fervently wished the house foundation were a foot higher than it actually was so that I could form a higher slope for quicker runoff flow, but that was not to be, of course. Some rainfall or melted snow always sat longer than I wanted in a few spots during all twelve years that I lived at this address. It became an unsolvable, but manageable, difficulty. As they say: You go with the flow. But in my case it was a slow flow.

Weathered boulders from an unneeded and decrepit wall on the easterly side of my land provided a support edging, and path marking, for the new oval planting mound in the center of the space. Flower colorings from both evergreen and deciduous shrubs, coupled with various bulbs and herbaceous perennials or annuals, were exclusively in a changing palette of red, pink, purple, lavender, and white. (As contrast, as well as to utilize the other colors of the spectrum, I planted the front and side garden areas with a focus on yellow, orange, blue, and white.)

Although the rear end of the property was originally evaluated as a somewhat "wild" section for my planting, I soon felt it needed more architectural definition at ground level to suit the rest of my design ideas. I then added railroad ties, but unused ones (the so-called industrial ties) without spike holes so they would not decay as fast, to supply a crisper front edge to the space while also providing a noticeable shadow line of interest with the adjacent lawn. The pathway behind the ties was simply an extension of the pine bark mulch used throughout the planting beds.

The first plantings in the raised, boulder-edged bed at the north end of the property.

Railroad-tie curbing adds crisp definition and a shadow line.

With this farthest-from-the-house section now under control, I turned to the hodgepodge of items located next to the house itself. An odd-shaped, not-very-useful terrace of precast cement pavers had nothing to recommend its continuance. The later addition of the cedar screen fencing, plus the inclusion of a few Canada hemlocks (*Tsuga canadensis*), further suggested a move toward a new terrace design. The area along the new cedar fence, which was more visible from the living room window and French doors, beckoned strongly for development of a more inviting outdoor sitting area. I agreed, particularly since a mature, wide-spreading apple tree nearby offered midday shading and a special focus worth enhancing.

In order to assure myself of the correct proportions for the new pavement when observed from all the compass directions, I outlined the intended dimensions with easily adjusted pieces of handy stones and some remnants of bamboo poles and fence palings. The break in the upper part of the outline redirected the eye toward the rear section of planting already in place.

After excavating the patchy grass and thin topsoil for reuse as fill material

The original hodgepodge at the rear of the house, as seen from the garage.

The addition of cedar fencing and a few screening Canada hemlocks (*Tsuga canadensis*) promoted a more inviting sitting area off the living room.

The odds and ends used to shape the outline for the new sitting space allowed easy adjustment.

later, I laid a 4-inch bed of sand as a uniform base for the relocated pavers—with bought additions to complete this enlarged layout—and added more railroad ties as raised barriers to keep the pavers from moving sideways. Because it seemed visually excessive to continue with pavement in the upper part of this lounging area, I returned to a cover of pine bark mulch, thus tying the area cohesively with the nearby pathway into the "wild" garden area.

To provide architectural emphasis here and to frame both the sitting area and the garden interest beyond it, a personally designed shelter was added the next year. Its construction became a high-budget item with a local carpenter. Special-order cedar posts formed the shelter's framework, while widely spaced cedar palings identical to the background fence provided the side and roof detailing, making an airy support for grape vines. The shelter anchored the middle space of this area with useful distinction. The screen backing appears solid at the top but more open at the bottom half. The upper portion became a screen with a skip-picket technique, alternating the palings on each side of the framework to allow space for vine growth through them. At the bottom half the skip-picket design was used on the sitting side only and thus allowed greater ventilation.

An unmortared stone wall alongside the cedar shelter used up the balance of the stones from my collapsed wall at the rear property line. It is free-standing of necessity due to the presence of a highly productive pear tree at the original ground level behind it, and I fully intended to maintain and enjoy the tree. This wall work consumed a goodly amount of my free time that season, but when completed it provided an attractive material relationship with the stone edging visible in the wild garden.

Untreated with any preservatives or stains, the cedar shelter naturally weathered within two years to a silver-tan coloring that matched the background fencing. This muted backdrop gave greater emphasis to my later addition of an in-ground, turquoise, fiberglass fountain basin, with its glistening water plume and soothing splash of sound throughout the summer and early autumn months. Electricity for the recirculating water pump, along with other capped outlets for use in serving hot food and drinks, was a simple matter of laying an underground power line in the planting bed next to the fence. Night lighting here was limited to the soft glow of candles with hurricane lamp shields on tables or hanging lanterns with candles strung from the shelter's roof. Far fewer insects bothered my guests with this subdued and soft-flickering illumination.

The sizable shelter and vine arbor anchor the sitting area.

Vines work their way up the shelter's palings, here viewed from the "wild" garden path.

Now that half of the rear garden was in a new, third-dimensional shape, I felt strongly that here the design treatment should be quite simple. To achieve that aim, I decided that an uncluttered carpet of lawn from the house to the rear of the lot was the best design solution since an unimpeded view can make any space seem longer than it actually is. To make it also appear wider, I broadened the grass area in a subtly enlarging cone-shape in its march toward the fine-textured planting selections in the rear garden space. This concept appeared workable in my mind, but it had to be field-tested with an actual layout.

After juggling a great number of different arrangements—again using the same movable props of remnant wood and stray bricks—in both curved and angular combinations, I finally settled on a somewhat contemporary, eye-pleasing composition. I also learned that my best evaluation of the ground design came with a clear overview taken from an upstairs window.

Railroad ties were again used to outline a gravel-based and bark-covered sitting area, but this time around they were positioned above the existing odd patch of grass to allow for additional soil fill that would move surface water as

Two years after construction, the now-weathered shelter gained a fountain.

Viewed from the upstairs window, the area near the garage was laid out using the same movable outline of wood and bricks.

The ever-present construction stockpile.

far as possible from the low-set house and direct it toward the dog-pen area behind the garage. This grading brought the tops of the ties flush with both the
gravel and soil backfill here and kept them from mixing. By midsummer, the
finished result was a highly rewarding prize for my efforts of several years.

My new garden spaces were blended smoothly into a cohesive whole by the
following spring. The total distance from the house to the rear planting backdrop measures only 100 feet, but it appears to be longer, and my guests were always surprised when they learn this tidbit of news. Much of this depth illusion
is attributable to leaving the central lawn panel unencumbered, to balancing
plant silhouettes and leafy textures in proper scale to each other, and to laying
the unifying lawn carpet to draw the eye farther along with ease. Even the muted
coloring of new outdoor furniture contributed subtly to the satisfying restful-
ness of the entire composition.

My final episode of translating the original mishmash at the house's rear

An overview from upstairs of the completed garage area in autumn.

into an end-to-end, useful completeness involved the addition of a contractor-built, 8-foot by 10-foot greenhouse. Attached to the north side of the building at the dining room set of windows, where winter sun happily managed to glide over the house roof to warm almost half of the greenhouse glass, this special feature incorporated the same shingle siding as the house for greater architectural unity and visual solidness. By this time the house and garage color had changed from white to mustard, which I found a lively and very agreeable coloring well suited to all manner of garden flowering and greenery. (Yes, I somehow managed to apply all the house paint myself, but I was younger, more energetic, and somewhat foolhardy then.)

Because the greenhouse area now needed a prominent entry walkway from the newly gated and fenced-off adjacent driveway, I decided it was time to upgrade the existing concrete pavers to an all-brick covering in a rosy tone. Choosing the great outdoor durability of a water-struck finish, I laid the brick on a

The new development's next spring season, as viewed from ground level.

sand base with tightly butted joints. For unity with the rest of the area I installed support curbing again of railroad ties, both flush-set and raised to suit the design conditions.

The brick-laying work proceeded slowly but surely over a few summer weekends, and then I was plagued by consistently wet periods for a whole month, which halted all activity to the point where it began to look like a "forever" project. This mess of incompleteness so close to the house, meant to be a prime connector to all other rear areas, became intolerable, and I was forced to hire a masonry contractor to dispel my frustration. This decision proved well worth the added expense since the talented work crew finished in a week what I had struggled valiantly to produce over a water-logged month. Brick coverage now extended from the driveway to the entry at the shelter, simplifying the number of surfaces throughout the garden. I was amazed to learn that the contractor had needed more than three thousand bricks to complete the expanded operation.

Now, after five years of on-again, off-again disturbance to the landscape, coupled with frequent necessary adjustments to my original vision of this garden

Construction of the greenhouse is underway at the now-mustard-colored house.

space's potential, the main elements were all finally in place. Even Rufus appeared as content and as much at home with the finished product as the owner on what was once just an uninspiring fragment of a suburban houselot. The outcome was definitely worth the long effort.

Rufus relaxes along the new brick paving at the completion of the project.

Metric Conversion Chart

TO CONVERT:	MULTIPLY BY:
Inches to centimeters	2.5
Feet to meters	0.3
Miles to kilometers	1.6
Square inches to square centimeters	6.5
Square feet to square meters	0.1
Acres to hectares	0.4

Index

Pages with photographs are indicated in italics.